Critical Acclaim for
THE CURMUDGEON RIDES AGAIN
****

"I'm not sure why we published it."
Matthew Clemens
President
Robin Vincent Publishing

"Dad, I did what you said. I read the book. It's okay."
Kevin Largent
Indianapolis, IN

"Largent's latest book is really average."
Richard Craig
Neighbor and
Presbyterian Minister

" ... if I was his editor at that newspaper he writes his columns for, I'd make him take a urine test."
Dr. Paul Sharp
Psychology Professor
Indiana University

"Remember. The profits from the sale of this book go to charity. That's the only thing that justifies buying it."
Prunella Pascal
Book Critic
Boston Journal

"Don't quit your day job."
God

"Don't laugh. I was his first grade teacher. I never dreamed he would get this far even."
Ms. Laverene Frank
Elementary Teacher (Ret.)
Mongo, IN

"I've just read *The Curmudgeon Rides Again*. I know of no better example to prove that we need to spend more money on education in this country."
George W. Bush
President

"After reading a couple of the example columns, I tried to stop the book from being printed. This is a consumer ripoff."
Ralph Nader
Consumer Advocate

"I taut dis was good stuff in some places ..."
Barney Critch
257936412
Jackson State Prison

"Read book. Wrote glowing review. Send the fifty dollars."
Shifty Paulson
Paulson's Review Service
Muncie, GA

"Simple, uncomplicated style. Reminds me of the kind of things my daughter wrote before she went into the first grade."
Mardell Stritch
Lewisburg, TN

THE CURMUDGEON RIDES AGAIN

A Perfect Bathroom Companion

By

R. KARL LARGENT

Award Winning Columnist

HERALD-REPUBLICAN

THE CURMUDGEON RIDES AGAIN – A Perfect Bathroom Companion
R. Karl Largent

Robin Vincent Publishing LLC
2829 Grand Avenue
Davenport, IA 52803

All rights reserved. The articles published herein have been reprinted by permission of Home News Enterprises, Inc, and no part of this book may be produced or transmitted in any form by any means, electronic, mechanical, photocopying, or otherwise, without the prior written permission of Home News Enterprises, Inc., the author and the publisher.

©2001 Robin Vincent Publishing LLC

First Printing: 2001

Library of Congress Control Number: 2001093054

ISBN: 0-9645606-4-X

CONTENTS

Foreword ix

Food, Fat and Other Aphrodisiacs 1

Chopsticks 101 or Where's the Meat 3
The Onion and Me 5
Me and V-8 8
Salad Bars – Dried Worms – and (choke) – Carrots .. 11
The Gift That Keeps On Annoying 13
Confessions Of An Addict 16
Introducing the LFS-1 19
Counting Calories and the Art of Self-Deceit 22

In China It's The Year Of The Septic Tank 25

I have an allergy. I'm allergic to work. 28
"What's your sign?" I said. 30
What do you send a sick florist? 33
I never had a penny to my name... 35
When you're down and out... 38
My wife missed her nap today 41
Walk into an antique store and say, "What's new?" .. 43
Things were rough when I was a baby. 46

My Wife Drives a Momserati 49

It ain't a fit night out for man nor beast. 52
How old would you be 54
If a man is a fool, the best thing to do 57
Saint: (noun) A dead sinner revised and edited. 59

I think I shall never see ...	62
...Where did we get the idea ...	64
By sudden and adroit movement ...	67
The very fact that we make such a to-do ...	70

A Tatterdemalion Testimony To Technology — 73

Writing is easy ...	76
I love being a writer.	79
My editor told me ...	81
One way I save energy ...	84
Television, like technology, feeds on itself.	87
The seat of the soul ...	90
I have a simple philosophy.	93

Machismo Is Not An Italian Cheese — 97

I only like two kinds of men ...	99
Margaret Mead on ...	101
It's not the men in my life that count ...	104
I like men to behave like men.	107
A man, being what he is, is likely to play games ...	109
A man will tell you that failing to be there ...	113
It's a scientific fact that if you ...	115

Irruoptop Is Potpourri Spelled Backwards — 119

Women want mediocre men ...	122
Authors are easy to get along with ...	124
If you can't say anything good about someone ...	128
It is said that there is one woman ...	130
When my cousin, Jerome, visits ...	133

God is not dead.	136
The urge to gamble is so universal ...	140

My Favorite Holiday Hasn't Been Invented Yet   143

The reason some men continue to smile ...	146
Guaranteed. If it's good, they'll stop making it.	148
Meetings are indispensable ...	151
My favorite toast ...	154
My advice is not to take life too seriously.	157
How can you whistle while you work ...	160
My wife is a good driver.	164

It's A Guy Thing   167

Love is a way with meaning for a woman.	170
The whole motivation for any man ...	172
To be a good politician ...	175
Is it hot in the coal mines?	178
I've never understood why people ...	181
Never eat at a place called Mom's.	185
The average man's opinions ...	189

One Last Thought   193

It's never as bad as you thought it would be.	195

FOREWORD

Old Yiddish proverb: "Man plans, God laughs." This should, of course, never be confused with that old stand-up line, "It's a small world ... but I wouldn't want to paint it."

I've been asked to write this Forward by the publisher in the form of a public apology for releasing this volume.

I am told Karl wrote all these columns between 1966 and 12:47 Eastern Standard Time. Like Ernest Hemingway he composed them while *standing* at his typewriter. But whereas the celebrated writer (that would be Ernest) did this as an outgrowth of his action persona, Karl merely likes to be ready to run if an irate reader comes to the door.

Still, Karl has soldiered his way through a number of life's rough spots. He learned early that the secret to young talent was the ability to exist without regular meals. This was further compounded when he married at a tender age, or as another Hoosier humorist (Kin Hubbard) once explained, "Two can live as cheaply as one, just not as long."

Unable to dance, Karl had measles as a child, he decided upon a career (writing) which involved as little movement as possible. Tough times taught him if you're not cynical, you're probably not paying attention. This is especially true if you write for a newspaper, because journalism breeds the motto: "If your mother says she loves you, check it out." Or, as one of Karl's favorite comedians (W. C. Fields) observed, "Trust everyone but always cut the cards."

Not surprisingly, Karl gravitated naturally towards a *Curmudgeon* writing style. Moreover, it had that funny C-sound – always an important part of any humorist's arsenal. On the other hand (hey, how many hands is that?), he always distrusted happy people — figuring they just couldn't have all the facts.

Still, Karl attempted to read all the right books, even if he got the wrong ideas out of them. And he tried to speak our language, though he often mispronounced it. Karl wanted to be a writer in the *worst* way ... which he has finally accomplished. Yet, as an old Indiana farmer once said, "Even a blind sow occasionally finds an ear of corn." So there are a few choice items to be rooted out here but nothing to write home about.

Surprisingly, Karl has not included my favorite insight of his, which he just shared with me yesterday – no, it was six years ago. Anyway, it went something like this: "Remember, when you're feeling so low you have to reach up to touch bottom ... whose bottom it is can make a big difference." Thanks, Karl.

—"Professor Wes" Gehring*

*Professor Wes is the author of many wonderful humor-related books (just ask his mom), such as the recent *Seeing Red: The Skelton in Hollywood's Closet*, which was also published by Karl's poor misguided press. When not writing, Gehring's day job has him teaching film comedy history (such as it is) at Ball State University.

Food, Fat and Other Aphrodisiacs

To paraphrase Bill Boldenbeck, "Food is a whole lot like sex: When it is good it is great, and even when it isn't all that good, it's not all that bad."

Turning to yet another of my boyhood idols, the foremost authority on pleasure-seeking activities, Sigmund Freud, the Father of Modern Psychiatry, is reported to have stated, "Food, like sex, for many is a pleasure seeking activity."

Well ... if the above cited gentlemen are anywhere near correct in their appraisal and assessment of food, I have been both a delectator and a wanna-be gormandizer for most of my life.

Proof of what I say? One only has to take into consideration the ponderous nature of my girth to see that I speak volumes of truth in this matter.

Why am I telling you all of this? Simple, I am compelled to do so. Besides, confession is good for the soul. By confessing my omnipresent fixation with food as well as my feelings of guilt every time I open a jar of peanut butter or reach for another Oreo cookie, I am acknowledging my human frailty.

Don't laugh. If you were raised Jewish, you know what I

mean. But you don't have to be raised in the Jewish faith to understand. Moral imperfection and feelings of guilt are part of growing up in the Catholic Church as well. If you grow up in the Catholic Church you are supposed to feel guilty about something some of the time (read that "everything, all of the time"). Feelings of guilt are an important dimension of the Catholic lifestyle. As Father Logan once said, "Show me a Catholic who doesn't feel guilty most of the time and I'll show you a Catholic who hasn't sufficiently digested the material in his catechism."

What other force could there possibly be for me to indulge in so many discourses on the subject of food, fat and other aphrodisiacs? Remember what Clement Freud said, "If you're one of those people who resolve to give up smoking, drinking, and loving, you won't actually live longer, but it will seem like it."

Chopsticks 101 or Where's The Meat?

Let me ask you a question. Do you dine out frequently? More specifically, every now and then do you and your significant other happen to encounter one of those fancy Japanese restaurants where they set you down at the same table with a bunch of folks you don't know? I mention Japanese restaurants because this is where it seems to happen most frequently.

Get the picture? Moonbeam and I happened to dine at one of those "get to know your fellow dinner partner" places the other night and I'm here to tell you the experience was less than gratifying.

First of all, I was seated next to a couple that were having a little spat. I assume this to be the case because she didn't talk to him. He didn't talk to her. Instead, he talked to me. Not good.

Why? Because I'm not much of a conversationalist. Especially at dinner. From the time I was a puppy, my parents preached that it was poor manners to talk with your mouth full. And ... when I'm eating, my mouth is usually full. Therefore I try to let others do most of the talking. And, generally speaking, I'm even less inclined to indulge in a little verbal give and take with a total stranger.

At any rate, I was busy wolfing my way through something that had been smeared back and forth over the grill a couple of times and topped off with an egg when the guy sitting beside me decided to introduce himself. He held out his hand, told me his name, and regaled me with more information about himself and his wife than even the IRS needs to know.

When I mumbled a couple of semi-incoherent responses it did not dampen his enthusiasm. If anything it seemed to spur him on. Finally he said with some disdain, "I notice you're eating with a fork."

"Lots of folks I know eat with forks," I replied.

"Not good Japanese food like this," he said, "... don't you know how to use chopsticks?"

With a mouthful of something I can't pronounce and having already been informed by my bride of 40 years that this Oriental repast was going to cost me $29 a plate, I admitted I had once tried to eat with chopsticks but had met with little success. "I never did get the food all the way up to my mouth and I went home hungry." Then I added, "... I do not consider that little episode the zenith of my dining career."

At this point, another equally vocal stranger (this one was sitting at the far end of the disjointed group and was perhaps even more annoying than the man sitting next to me) offered to give me a lesson in eating with chopsticks. More interested in eating than learning, I waved him off. "I'll stick with the fork," I informed him, "... my mother taught me to eat with a fork when she thought I was old enough not to poke myself in the eye and incur facial trauma." Then I added, "... forks aren't bad once you get the hang of them."

Obviously rebuffed, the erstwhile chopstick instructor went back to his meal and for a whole 30 seconds (maybe not that long) everyone dined in silence. I viewed this little interlude as a marvelous opportunity to sift through all the unrecognizable things the Japanese chef had dumped on my plate. I had cataloged my way through bean sprouts, carrots with a thyroid condition, bamboo thingies, and old bird nests when I thought I recognized something that looked like a piece of meat. As I probed deeper into the origins of this mystery substance, the guy sitting next to me informed me he had always been a vegetarian. "Half of this country's health problems can be attributed to the fact that we eat too much meat," he said.

Since the man in question had a prominent wart on his nose, I decided to reply to his little snit by informing him that my mother told me the only people who had warts on their noses were vegetarians. He shook his head, assumed a rather sullen demeanor and became silent.

At that point, I asked the fellow sitting next to me if he knew Chopstick Master at the end of the table. When he admitted he hadn't been introduced, I pulled off the coup of the evening. I saw to it that the two men introduced themselves to each other.

"That was nice of you," Moonbeam cooed, "... you usually aren't that sociable."

"Sociable has nothing to do with it," I grunted. "I just want them to leave me alone so I can eat."

"Are you going to try to use the chopsticks?" she said.

I shook my head. "No way, if I'm lucky enough to find that piece of meat again I intend to stab it with my fork before it runs off and hides again."

The Onion and Me

Are you an onion fan?

I am. But ... I don't know how I got to be that way.

When other kids on the block were wolfing down peanut butter and jelly sandwiches, I was tooling around the family kitchen indulging in my own gastronomic delight, peanut butter and onion sandwiches.

Fifty years later I'm still doing it.

The best palate-pleasing combination I've come up with so far is white potato bread, real butter, several thin slices of onion (preferably Vidalia), and a layer of smooth (if I say "Creamy and smooth" will you know what brand I'm talking about?) pea-

The Curmudgeon Rides Again

nut butter.

(Cooking tip: Don't slather on so much peanut butter that you overpower the presence of the onion.)

Looking back, I've always been a big onion eater. It doesn't matter what kind; I love onions on everything. I put onions on all my sandwiches, mix them in my scrambled eggs, make sure Moonbeam puts an ample amount in with the roast, load onions in my salads, and I plumb revel in a cup of baked onion soup topped off with cheese and croutons.

Despite my overwhelming affection for this epicurean delight (by definition, it's a bulb) that comes from the Middle East, my passion for onions has, on occasion, impacted my social life.

Back in my high school days (before beginning my career as a Curmudgeon), I had trouble getting dates. Luwanda Frump wouldn't go to the movies with me because she said I smelled like onions all the time. Try as I might, I could not understand why she considered this a negative. She obviously had no idea how many onions I had to eat to achieve my odoriferous goal.

On the football team they would never let me stand in the huddle with the rest of the team. My nickname was O. J. ; O. J. stood for "Onion Juice."

Not well known is the fact that many famous people have carried on a love affair with onions. Gen. George Custer used to sit on his bunk when he was a cadet at West Point and eat onions like apples. If you've ever read anything about Custer, you know he was pretty much a loner when he was at the Academy.

Tershweld Lum, the famous lawyer and blacksmith, admittedly best known as being the inventor of cheap wine, was a big booster of the onion. His close friend, Prankmore Lolly, the man who developed the paper bag, was also a noted onion fan. Lolly and Lum were famous for sitting on the steps of the local court house eating onions and drinking cheap wine concealed in a paper sack, while they commented on the weather and the price of cheap candy.

Onion aficionados, unlike the folks who embrace and espouse other passion fruits, appear to be oblivious to the fact that onions are actually considered a health food. It's a fact, onions contain a hormone-like substance called prostaglandin (pronounced "prostaglandin") that can lower blood pressure and thin the blood, thereby fighting clotting and heart disease. Onion lovers say they love onions because they taste good and because the aroma of onions is a sexual turn-on. It has been said that if you give the onion lover a big juicy Vidalia onion they will revert to a behavior akin to that of a prancing goat at a drive-in movie.

Unfortunately, all too often, this is where cultures clash. Take a woman who considers a man's best friend to be a bottle of Listerine and pair her with a man who considers an onion souffle to be a repast fit for a king and you have the makings of a rocky relationship.

So where does this leave us? I want to encourage onion eaters ... openly and enthusiastically ... to come out of the closet. Everyone knows you are in there. (They can smell you.) Embrace and rejoice. Onions have long been known for their congestion clearing properties when people have colds. And, while there are no long term university studies to verify onion lovers' claims, onions are believed to clear up pimples, cure most scalp diseases, and shorten IRS audits.

True, experts recommend eating onions raw to achieve maximum health benefits. Onions that have been cooked, sauteed, baked, blanched, fried, or breaded, actually do less to satisfy the taste buds of the true onion lover. If someone tells you they like onion rings, they are as much as admitting that they are sissy onion eaters.

Onions make a terrific gift for any holiday. This Valentine's Day give onions. What could be more rewarding? Imagine the joy on children's faces when they scurry about looking for those colorful Easter onions. Or ... better yet, how about an onion cake for Christmas?

Or is that carrying it a bit too far?

Me and V-8

When Moonbeam travels she leaves instructions around the house to make certain things work smoothly in her absence.

Let me give you an example.

Moonbeam is very thorough about this little ritual. By the time my bride has departed on one of her adventures, the doors on the majority of our kitchen cabinets are covered with charts, memos, battle plans, reminders, directions and her blueprints for the old Curmudgeon's healthy living.

From the nonchalant way you are reacting to this news about what amounts to my bride's blatant tendency toward being a control freak, this behavior apparently makes sense to you. But what would you say if I told you she sticks those little yellow sticky notes on mirrors, the dashboard, on my pillow, the back door, the refrigerator, and even the lid on the john. (Note: She never places these notes on the dishwasher or washing machine because she knows that when I go near either of these two appliances, I break out in a stress rash.)

All of my bride's efforts are designed, obviously, to get me through her absence without me having to dial 911.

I know what you're thinking. You're thinking I sound like I don't appreciate all the extra effort my bride puts into making certain things run smoothly in her absence. If I don't sound overly appreciative it may well be that I think she often goes far beyond a demonstration of wifely care and concern. Take last week ... Freight Train (our 80 pound Black Lab) and [...] uled to go on a diet and the light of my married li[fe ...] Mexico.

First there were the detailed instructions, [a ...] check list, by date and time, on both the amount and frequency of medicine to give to the dog. Each time I accomplished this somewhat Herculean task (Have you ever tried to give an 80 pound dog a suppository?) I was required to initial the chart with both the time and date.

Then there was the matter of making certain I stayed on my diet while my bride was out of town. This required two charts. First I had to read Chart A to determine the components of each meal. A typical meal might read something like one unit of starch, three units of meat, two vegetable units and one fruit unit. Pretty simple, huh?

No way. Because before you can go any further with your meal plans, you have to determine what a "unit" is.

You have to understand something about following a diet when your wife is a nurse. You can't just read one chart and dig in. Part of their madness is to keep you (the dieter) confused. You have to refer to Chart B which tells you how you can exchange items you don't have in the cupboard on Chart A for items that you might have in the cupboard that are on Chart B.

Still with me?

Chart B (on the cabinet door) refers you to Chart C inside the lid of the freezer. Chart C is a guide to what's in the freezer. Inside the freezer there are a number of small cartons containing foods of various varieties ... all of which correspond to some food group in the diet. Carton 1, for example, contains chicken breasts. According to the writing on the carton, each chicken breast is equivalent to three units. I'm not sure how this works because some chickens have bigger breasts than others.

There are three other categories of cartons in the freezer as well. Cartons marked 2 are beef, each cut in three ounce portions. Carton 3 is turkey. Carton 4 is seafood. Carton 5 is some kind of meat substitute that tastes like the mystery meat I used to get when I was stationed in the Arctic. My goal in life is never again to get hungry enough that I would be willing to eat anything that comes out of a carton with the number 5 on it.

Still with me?

OK, having selected a 3-unit serving from a 3 carton, I now check off (in another chart on another door of another kitchen cabinet) the vegetable requirement. This is the revolting part of the diet and at the same time, the easy part. Why is it revolting? I don't like vegetables. So, I disregard the vegetable tray and trundle back to the refrigerator for the V-8 juice. (Note: If you have a vivid imagination you can lace your V-8 with an ounce or so of Worcestershire sauce and delude yourself into thinking your diet includes Bloody Marys.)

Don't go away. We're not done yet.

Now we have to come up with a unit of fruit. It took a long time for Moonbeam to convince me that a wedge of lemon pie was not an acceptable substitute for my fruit unit. To determine what is an acceptable substitute for fruit, we journey to another cupboard and another chart. I dig the applesauce, but that is two units instead of one and Moonbeam isn't here to divide up the applesauce. She does not trust me to make such adjustments.

Finally, we're down to the bread. This I can handle. A bread is a bread. Right?

Wrong. It can't be a "white" bread. It has to be a "dark" bread. But with a healthy measure of guile and cunning I have solved this little dilemma; I toast the "white" bread. Now it's "dark."

As I sit here, I'm wishing Moonbeam would come home.

This healthy eating stuff is more than I want to deal with. One from Chart A or two from Chart B unless it's a meatless day means I'm supposed to turn to Column 2 on Chart C and refer to the alternative choices on Chart A. Come on.

Pass the peanut butter.

Salad Bars – Dried Worms – and (choke) – Carrots

I like salad bars ... particularly the fancy and creative ones. One of my favorite salad bars is in Davenport, Iowa. All the salad fixings are in the back of a Model T pickup truck. That's almost as creative as the one in St. Louis where they put everything in an old bathtub.

My favorite salad bars are the ones that have lots of stuff on them in addition to the vegetables. To my way of thinking, a really great salad bar offers several flavors of pudding and red Jell-O. Red Jell-O is probably my favorite thing on salad bars. I used to spoon down a healthy ration of Jell-O and tell my mother I ate a lot of salad.

The only real problem I have with salad bars (other than the fact they are usually cluttered with vegetables) is that I don't always know what I'm eating. For example, what are those things that look like dried worms? They are curvy like worms. They are wrinkled like worms. They are even brown like worms. The other day I popped one in my mouth without the benefit of the other salad components to hide the taste. It tasted awful. To my knowledge I've never actually eaten worms, but if I ever do I'm pretty sure I already know what the worm would taste like.

One day I tried a spoonful of those little brown things that are supposed to look like bits or bites of bacon. I ate them without the salad just to see what they tasted like. They tasted awful too. They may even taste worse than the things that look like dried worms.

All of this leads me to ask, why do things that taste so bad by themselves taste good when you mix them all up in a salad? I think the person who invented salad realized that her invention didn't have much going for it and that's why she invented salad dressing. Salad dressings sorta cover up the fact that the rest of the stuff is pretty blah.

Have you noticed that a really good salad bar always has lots of crocks of stuff? I'm not an authority on "expression derivation" but that's probably where the expression "that's a crock" comes from.

I saw a salad bar once that had all the salad makings in glass bowls. People were ignoring that salad bar. I think it's because for once they could actually see what they were eating when they ate a salad. Crocks hide what the stuff really looks like. To show you what I mean, once I even ate raw broccoli. The crock sort of disguised it. The crock couldn't disguise the carrots though. I don't think they should put carrots on salad bars. Carrots are for horses and rabbits.

I think my aversion to carrots comes from the fact my mother (the Democrat) used to make me eat lots of carrots when I was a puppy. "Don't you want to have good eyesight?" she would say. Sure I wanted good eyesight, but I didn't want it bad enough to eat carrots.

My parents were never quite able to get their story together on this carrots and eyesight thing. As a result, I was never really convinced you had to eat carrots to be able to see well. My father always told me owls could see at night and that the eagle had the best sight of all. All of which, to me at least, proves that the carrot's contribution to good eyesight is over rated. Ask yourself, have you ever seen an owl or an eagle eat a carrot?

When I used to ask my mother about this eagle and carrot thing, she would say, "Shut up and eat your carrots."

But back to the salad bars. Have you ever wondered why they don't put the names on the handles of the spoons in the vegetables like they do the handles on the spoons in the salad dressing? I mean, wouldn't you like to know it was marinated spinach instead of what it really looks like?

Lately I've noticed some of the salad bars have crocks of seeds sitting at one end of the salad bar. Aren't you just a little bit curious what kind of seeds are in those crocks? Most of the seeds are pretty small. It seems to me like it would be a better idea to plant the seeds and let them grow up into something big enough to feed several people. It may well be that folks in some of those underfed countries would have more to eat if we weren't eating all those seeds on our salad bars.

Truth is, even though I don't know what kinds of seeds I'm eating, I put lots of them on my salad. It makes my salad crunchy, more substantial ... sorta like I'm getting more for my money.

One of the restaurants in our town has several different kinds of food bars. There is a salad bar, a desert bar, a seafood bar, a regular bar, and something they call a fun bar. I don't go to this particular restaurant very much. The last time I was there they had carrots in the Jell-O.

The Gift That Keeps On Annoying

What could be more insidious, more contriving, more Machiavellian, than giving a person a calorie counter for their birthday?

Let me explain. There we were, staring wantonly at a chocolate-frosted, double decked devil's food birthday cake with enough candles to alarm the local fire marshal when Sadistic Daughter (our youngest) hands me a vest pocket guide to gastronomic deprivation.

Like Pagliaccio, I was laughing on the outside and vowing to get even on the inside. But then I began reading this epistle of discontent. Four pages into the dastardly document I gave up all hope of ever being anything except the local tubbo.

Take my word for it. The world of calorie counting is not steeped in logic. Nor is it logical the way people who write about calories approach the subject. To break this whole subject of calories down into something you and I can understand, I want you to think of a calorie as a glob of fat about the size of a golf ball. Ergo, a dozen calories are a dozen golf balls.

The first thing you need to understand is something called calorie behavior. The first rule of calorie behavior is this: When you consume a calorie it goes immediately to a place on your body where it will be most noticeable. To illustrate, an order of biscuits and gravy is tantamount to consuming and hoping no one notices the approximately 600 golf balls you have just wolfed down and are now enhancing the overall size of your love handles.

Mashed potatoes and gravy, no matter how little you consume, are equal to another chin.

Lobster with butter is good for a whole new assortment of dimples in cellulite city.

The misdirected folks who published this little guide actually want you to believe there are only four basic food groups. Actually there are 64 food groups. Want proof? They do not tell you that the milk and milk products food group does not include a chocolate milkshake. To find the calorie value (think golf balls) of a chocolate milkshake you have to look in the section entitled, "Hey, Fat Person, This Is What You Can't Have."

In the meat, eggs, fish, and poultry group, you have to choose between steak (a 12-ounce T-bone is about 1,600 golf balls) and an egg (80 golf balls) or 57 different kinds of cheese ... or fish. Among the cheeses, a tablespoon of cottage cheese is 17 calories and a brick of American is 389 golf balls. All of which, if you are serious about this dieting stuff, makes you ask, "How big is a brick?" Think about it; a brick of cheese probably doesn't weigh as much as gold brick. It may cost as much though.

The third food group, vegetables and fruits, is equally confusing. The average beet is 21 golf balls. Why? It's my contention that anything that tastes as bad as a beet ought to be negative calories. Now this is where this calorie counting business falls apart. That same beet, diced and drained is now 29 calories. How come? Where did those other eight calories come from? This is the kind of misinformation that makes me distrust people who talk about calories.

The fourth food group is bread and cereal. Calories (Are you still thinking "golf balls?") in this food group vary all over the place. But once again, there is a way to reduce all this confusing calorie counting to something meaningful. Apply this simple test. With breads and cereals, if it tastes good, it is fattening. If it tastes bad, it is still fattening but you won't eat as much of it.

Apparently some food items are loaded with hidden calories. Example: If you eat a pigeon you consume 650 calories. If you cook it, it adds another 100 calories. Here the question is, why would they even list squab raw?

On the other hand if you like to think and talk about calories (Is it more or less painful to think of them as golf balls?) and who doesn't ... a handbook like this is invaluable. For example, it informs you that one pound of fat is equivalent to 3,500 calories or golf balls. Actually, if you tell someone you are 20 pounds overweight it really doesn't sound all that bad unless you are only

2'4" tall. However, if you tell them you are 70,000 golf balls over the limit, they will look at you with unbridled disgust and are likely to tell you that you need help.

The rule here is you have to burn 500 more calories than you take in each day to lose a pound a week. Which means that given the magnitude of my weight problem I can achieve my weight loss goal by the year 2047.

At the back of the book there is a chart. It contains the average daily allowable calorie intake depending on height, weight, and life style. According to the chart I would not be overweight if I were 14 inches taller and ran 27 miles each day.

After careful calculation and much consideration I worked out a menu that will get me less than 2,000 calories a day. With my new diet I can have an artichoke, a bean sprout, one leaf of escarole, one clove of garlic, some horseradish, a kumquat, an onion, a pepper, one stalk of rhubarb, a tablespoon of sauerkraut, some tea-vinegar, and watercress twice a day.

Hey, if that doesn't overwhelm your palate with culinary anticipation, what will?

By now you are probably asking yourself why I don't just accept the way I am and let it go at that. The truth is I'm trying to help Moonbeam avoid the long legal shadow that has been cast over our marriage the past several years. The plain truth is there is enough to make two of me in one body. If I can't find a way to get rid of one of me, they may charge Moonbeam with bigamy.

Confessions Of An Addict

They say confession is good for the soul. If that's the case, my soul is rejoicing. I am about to come out of the closet. Well ... actually, it's not really a closet ... it's actually more like a

Food, Fat and Other Aphrodisiacs

factory ... a chocolate factory.

Coming out, revealing that is, some deep, dark, guarded secret about something you've long been taught to be ashamed of, is difficult. In the painful process of disclosure you ask yourself an endless string of soul-searching questions like, will my children ever speak to me again? Will the community turn their back on me? Will the pastor (from the pulpit) refer to me as an example of what can happen when an otherwise normal, God-fearing man yields to temptation? Will my co-workers look at me with veiled ridicule?

The risk of coming out is enormous. My job(s) may be at stake, my reputation ruined, income shut off, my very means of survival may even be in jeopardy. Even so, I feel compelled to make this potentially career-shattering admission. I (dare I say it?) am a (gulp) chocoholic.

There, I've said it.

Have I lost your respect? Will you speak to me when we pass on the street? Or will you avert your eyes, pretending to be distracted by a colorful display of clothes hangers at the local dry cleaner? Rather than acknowledge my presence will you find it more compelling to contemplate the various kinds of kosher ketchup at Kuznetsk's delicatessen?

No matter what the consequences, I cannot go back. Yes ... I am an addict. One day I was a normal, happy child, frolicking my way through life, obsessed with my James Bond secret agent decoder ring (straight out of a Wheaties box) and my autographed picture of Andy Rooney. The next I had been pulled into my sinister playmate's (Alvin Wade) backyard and amidst dire threats to never whisper a word of this to my mother, I was given my first taste of (gulp) chocolate.

Instant hooko.

"What is this stuff?" I demanded.

Alvin curled his lip, glanced about to make certain no one

could overhear him. "It's fudge," he hissed, his voice barely above a sibilation, "... double rich milk chocolate with almonds. My mom makes it."

At that very moment the age of innocence began slithering away. "More," I pleaded.

That night, as my mother (the Democrat) urged me to say my prayers before I climbed into bed, I had a terrible feeling she knew. "Is there something you want to tell me?" she asked.

I shook my head. That was the first lie. In the weeks that followed I quickly built upon my new life of deceit. At Thompson's store I used my lunch money to buy Hershey bars. Down at the fire station where we hung out after school, I found myself doing small chores for the firemen to make money to buy more chocolate cupcakes.

At school, when the school had an Oreo cookie sale to help defray the costs of purchasing new band uniforms, I didn't sell my cookies; I ate them. I told Sister Rosemary Elizabeth Fern June Lois Barbara Twyla Mary (Did you ever notice how long nuns' names are?) that I had been mugged in the alley by a 23-foot-tall, 4,000-pound chocolate-eating gorilla wearing a Notre Dame sweatshirt.

Sister said she didn't believe me. Looking back, I suppose I went too far when I said the gorilla was wearing a Notre Dame shirt, huh?

Each day I slipped further into my addiction. I had to have chocolate. I would do anything for chocolate. Even work. When I was in high school I took a job at a soda fountain just so I could be near chocolate. The owner of the drugstore fired me when he caught me laying on my back under the chocolate dispenser and letting the syrup drip into my mouth.

I had lost control. I put chocolate on everything. Chocolate sandwiches. Fresh garden salads with chocolate dressing.

Chocolate casseroles. When Lent came, Sister wanted us all to give up meat. I did it gladly. I still had chocolate.

How bad has it become? I have hidden chocolate in the garage, behind the john, in my closet, under the bed. Once, when I was older, I even had a supply stashed behind my mother's picture of President Kennedy on the TV in the living room. If she had known, I don't know which would have bothered her more: the fact that I had this obsession with chocolate or that a registered Republican got that close to her picture of JFK.

It has never seemed to make much difference — fudge, chocolate cake, chocolate milk, candy bars, Turtles, chocolate ice cream, Oreo cookies — it all works. Drug stores, truck stops, supermarkets, right in plain view like theater lobbies ... I've got my sources.

Is it too late? Am I too old, too wily, too cagey? Am I beyond help?

Relief!

So there it is. Now you know. I've confessed. Does my soul feel relieved because I have finally stepped out of the shadows of deceit and admitted my addiction?

Yup.

Sure does.

Pass that can of Hershey's syrup. I need a drink.

Introducing the LFS-1

Today's word is "lipo." Lipo comes to us from the Greek word *lipos*, which has nothing to do with the Chinese poet, Li Po, who wandered around the rice paddies 2,000 years ago mumbling catchy verses about overweight dragons.

Lipo is also the front end of a word that refers to a hot

The Curmudgeon Rides Again

medical procedure called liposuction. For the edification of you skinny folk, liposuction to us fat packers is the medical equivalent to being "born again."

Liposuction is just exactly what it sounds like ... a medical procedure for removing excess fatty tissue from places where most folks don't want excess fatty tissue. Think about it. Now there is a way. After all the jogging has worn out your $200 jogging shoes, the rigid diets have left you with a burning desire to put out a hit contract on your dietitian, and you have grown tired of looking like the "before" picture on the poster at the health club, liposuction may be your answer.

Just the other day I waddled into the bathroom and clawed my way up on the scale to see who was winning the suet derby. Unfortunately, I was. If your scale files a protest every time you get on it ... there is hope.

Are you like me? Despite your diet, you notice with dismay that certain parts of you are not going away. (Eat your heart out, Li Po.) Does it look like there is a tube of summer sausage wrapped around my waistline?

It's a fact, reducing the old calorie intake and rigorous exercise (two pushups a day) will tighten the trapezius, but more than likely the old "spare tire" just doesn't go flat. Conclusion, the answer to ample adipose may well be liposuction.

In seeking a liposuction solution to your sebaceous silhouette, you quickly learn that medicos adept at restoring the svelte self, are hard to find. And when you do locate one, you soon discover that they charge a good deal more for their services than the cat that hammered out the dings on your family fliver. My friends, this is body work of a whole different nature.

So — what's the solution? Don't despair fellow blubber butts and thunder thighs. If you're tired of carrying around an entire spare percussion section in your Bugle Boy jeans, hope is on the way. It's called "you-do-it" liposuction, and it comes to

Food, Fat and Other Aphrodisiacs

you in the privacy of your own home.

This handy little device is called the LFS-1. The LFS stands for Little Fat Sucker. It is shipped completely assembled with three (count them) "excess extractors" — small, medium, and industrial strength.

The makers of LFS-1 claim that ugly cellulite can be completely eliminated often in as few as a few sessions (See warranty statement for definition of "few"). For you guys, that brochure claims that beer bellies can come off in minutes (See warranty section for how many minutes). With the LFS-1, all you cute little corpulents out there can be fit and trim in virtually no time at all.

And ... that's not all. This marvelous instrument doesn't stop with just the liposuction feature. For an astonishingly low price of $19.95 (plus S&H) you also receive a two color, 24-page brochure that teaches you not only how to get rid of unsightly blubber but how to use this amazing appliance in dozens of other hard-to-perform chores around the house. For example, by simply attaching the "extender" to your LFS-1 you can get that last bit of jelly out of the jar and clean out the grease traps under your kitchen sink.

BUT ... That's not all.

If you act now, the makers of the LFS-1 will send you an assortment of skin-colored patches to plug and cover those unsightly little holes in your body where you have applied the Fat Sucker. No one, not even your closest friends, will know your secret to the new, fitter, trimmer, more appealing you. These handy little skin colored patches also act as an instant access cover for those quick little "tidy up" sessions. If you're going out for the evening, a brief, 30-second LFS "quickie" instantly reduces your garment size by up to two full inches. Just remove the access patch, plug in the LFS-1 and let it suck.

And now, just in time for the holidays, the company is

offering the new LFS-1A model for anorexics. This enables you to pass on the fat you removed to someone who can really use it.

Hurry, supplies are limited.

No C. O. D.'s please.

Counting Calories and the Art of Self-Deceit

I ran across a distressing piece of information the other day. Someone sent me a report that said heredity had nothing to do with being fat. If that's the case, I can no longer continue my life-long practice of blaming my ancestors for my rather pronounced corpulent appearance.

In other words, my fleshy spare tire has nothing to do with the shape of my father's brothers, my Uncle Ferndock or my mother's Aunt Lardacious. My portly posture, according to what I read, has to do solely with keeping track of what I eat, not carefully counting calories, and the aforementioned practice of self-deceit.

For a long time now I have stoutly maintained that I have had some sort of glandular problem, i.e., no matter how hard I worked or how little I ate, there was a Machiavellian flaw in my calorie-burning mechanism.

Wrongo, say the experts. When people don't lose weight even though they say they are dieting, either the diet or the way they are monitoring their intake is fatally flawed. These flaws are most likely due to short memory (remembering everything you ate during a given period), poor arithmetic skills (inability to accurately total up calorie intake), and basic self-deceit (example: a willingness to view French Fried Zucchini as the vegetable for a given meal).

Hey, my memory isn't all that good, I'll admit it. It's difficult for me to recall, with any degree of accuracy, just exactly how many Oreo cookies I consumed yesterday (How many are in a package?). By the same token I can't recall how many carrots I ate yesterday either ... or was that last week?

So, in order to offset the impact of a deteriorating memory, this article suggests that dieters carry a pad and pencil with them so they can write it down anytime they eat something. On paper that sounds good, but if my memory is the problem, how am I going to remember the paper and pencil?

I don't believe inaccurate calorie count is my problem either. If I can remember what I ate, I can always go back and count the calories. The real problem seems to be coming reasonably close to the caloric value of a given item. Was that a "big" french fry or a "small" french fry?

Therein lies an example of the quandary calorie counters face. A small milkshake, according to my pocket size calorie counter is 350 calories. A giant milkshake is 550 calories. This means that a giant milkshake is not twice as big as a small. It is, however, larger than a "regular," which isn't listed in my book, but which is the smallest size my favorite ice cream store offers.

What's a dieter to do?

I call the "regular" a "small" and applaud myself for not ordering a "giant."

This basic self-deceit dimension of my character is not necessarily a flaw either. You must understand that self-deceit is an important part of the homo-sapien's self-esteem mechanism. Ask yourself, what good does it do an unfortunate individual to stand in front of a full-length mirror and say, "Good grief! No one human being ever looked so bad." You know, as well as I, that our egos can't take that kind of honesty. Instead we say, "Hey, if I shed a pound here and a pound there, I won't look so bad."

True, that may be self-deceit, but it allows the individual to have hope. Doesn't it?

True, such fallacious statements can be dangerous. But, I contend a little self-deceit is better than a total systems collapse which may trigger a thought that goes something like, "Go ahead and pig out, I'm beyond hope."

By now you are probably asking yourself, just exactly how do these so-called diet experts compensate for the mental gymnastics we anti-anorexics go through in calculating our daily calorie intake? It's simple. They have devised an ingenious device called "the box." "The box" is, in reality, nothing more than a 9-by-12 room with all kinds of electronic monitoring devices in it.

The overweight individual is incarcerated in this (let's call it what it actually is, a cell) and food is made available through little slits in the wall. The person is informed how many items he has eaten and the actual calorie count of each item and asked to record both.

Supposedly this is an honor system and at the end of the 24-hour period, the person (inmate/guinea pig/test subject) must report their (his/her/its) estimated intake. The fat watchers then know whether the individual has the aforementioned bad memory, poor math skills, or practices self-deceit. After they know that, they can counsel the fat person accordingly. Some system, huh?

Hmmmmm. Hand me that pack of butter cookies. I want to think about this.

In China It's The Year Of The Septic Tank

A number of years ago, I decided to return to school in order to pursue a graduate degree in writing. As I recall, it was a rather tightly structured curriculum which permitted few opportunities for the student to explore electives. One of the possibilities, however, was a three-hour course on Chinese culture.

Because the Soviet Union had recently collapsed and I was then starting a new two-book contract ... a task which required me to continue the theme of a Communist threat to the free world, the class came at a most opportune time. Some sixteen weeks later, with volumes of lecture notes and five or six books on China in tow, I began to write *Red Tide*. But, as they say, that's another story.

Most of our class discussion and many of our lectures pertained to the social, economic, and political structure in modern-day China. Even so, there were any number of occasions when I drifted off into the warped recesses of the right side of my brain to find that the grim portrait most Americans have of the Chinese is a bit too baleful. True, they are industrious. True, they

The Curmudgeon Rides Again

are numerous. And, true, they are practical.

Take the Chinese perspective on the horoscope. Here in America, astrology is pretty complicated. Our horoscopes have three influences: the zodiac, the houses, and the planets. That's a lot of influences.

For us, the Zodiac consists of 12 divisions or signs. The houses (there are 12 of these dudes as well) all of which supposedly influence a certain part of a person's life (like their personality). Then the planets get involved to really complicate things. Pretty confusing, huh?

Not the Chinese. The Chinese zodiac is straight to the point. None of this "sign of Leo" or you are an "Aries" nonsense. In the Chinese zodiac you are a Tiger, or an Ox, or a Dragon, or something like that. There is no pussy footing around, they call a spade a spade (actually none of the signs are called a "spade" ... but you get the point).

The last time I checked there were close to five billion Chinese. That's a lot of Chinese. Think how difficult it would be for them to prepare an astrological chart for five billion people if they had a complicated horoscope like ours.

If you think about it, I feel certain you'll agree with me. The Chinese horoscope gets right to the meat of the matter. If you were born in 1960, 1972, 1984, (12 year increments) you are, plain and simple, "a Rat." Hey, we all know what a rat is don't we? The Chinese boil being a Rat down to the fact that even though they are ambitious and honest, Rats tend to be unwise with money and they don't make lasting friendships (sounds like a girl I used to date).

According to the Chinese zodiac I am a "Dog." Therefore I am loyal, honest, work well with others and am generous. I think that's probably the way others would describe me. The "Dog" according to the Chinese is also "somewhat stubborn" and "often selfish."

In China It's The Year Of The Septic Tank

I guess they can't be right about everything.

P.S.   You will note that I begin each piece (it seems a bit pompous to call them "essays" or "columns" ... after all, they are no longer in column form) with Henny Youngman's one liners. I'm a big Henny Youngman fan and a sucker for corny jokes. Besides, I couldn't think of any other way to work them into whatever we are going to call this exercise.

"I have an allergy. I'm allergic to work."
Henny Youngman

My father had two favorite sayings regarding behavior. The first was, "There is no excuse for rudeness." The second was, "Never say anything that will hurt someone's feelings." My bride of forty some years, Moonbeam, has her own version of that second dictum, which is, "If you can't say something kind, try not to say anything at all."

Now I don't know about the rest of the country, but if you hail from parts here and abouts, you've heard things like this all your life. We are almost as mannerly as those folks from Mississippi. All of which makes me think that if I talk about what I'm going to talk about, people will think I'm being unkind.

Actually, it's not so much my problem as much as it is our dog's problem. Our dog is Maggie and Maggie has a sorry case of halitosis. To put it a little more straightforward, Maggie has some of the worst morning (actually it hangs around all day) breath I've ever encountered. Admittedly, this would not be a problem if Maggie was aloof and stand offish like Sadistic Daughter's cat. But, Maggie isn't. Our girl, Maggie, is one of those up in your face, "... boy oh boy you look like a human and humans pet dogs" kind of pooch.

The other evening we had a small social gathering at our abode and the conversations of eight people came to an abrupt halt when Maggie opened her mouth to yawn. The people all started looking at each other like someone in the room had severe gastro-intestinal problems. By the time the air cleared, three people had excused themselves to go to the powder room.

We have tried everything with Maggie. We have changed her diet, laced her water with Listerine and put perfume on her

In China It's The Year Of The Septic Tank

Purina. Nothing works. When Maggie barks, flowers wilt. When she pants, odious smells waft through the house as though we had a malfunctioning garbage disposal. Pastor Good was paying us a visit the other night when Maggie breathed on him. His eyes rolled back in his head, he folded his hands and prayed for ten solid minutes. I'm convinced he thought Moonbeam and I had buried something unsavory under the house.

Someone suggested we teach Maggie to chew gum. I tried that. It didn't work. She swallowed the gum. On another occasion I held one hand on the top of her muzzle, moved it up and down and held my other hand under her chin trying to teach her to chew. That didn't work either.

Moonbeam, being a nurse, tells me that most bad breath emanates from the stomach. If that's the case, it wouldn't help to teach her to brush her teeth because the problem goes deeper than that. Do you suppose it would help to have her stomach pumped?

For awhile I thought it might be something she was eating when she went out in the woods. So I followed her. What I learned is that she isn't eating other animals when she is out there because I saw a skunk, two raccoons, a squirrel and two deer. They all ran when they saw Maggie coming.

We tried making Maggie stay outdoors but the neighbors complained. One neighbor lady stood on her back porch the other morning, sniffed a couple of times after we put Maggie out and promptly called the man to come clean her septic tank.

Last week Moonbeam called a firm in Chicago that makes gas masks. The gas mask man told her his deluxe model would filter out anything. When Moonbeam gave the man shipping instructions he said, "You wouldn't happen to be the people who have the dog with bad breath would you?" When Moonbeam asked him how he had heard about Maggie, he told us seven of our neighbors had ordered their deluxe gas masks as well.

One new fellow in our neighborhood got a whiff of our dog, called, and asked me to quit burning tires. The way it's been going we'll be hearing from the Environmental Protection Agency any day now. I wonder how much we can be fined if our dog's breath violates the Federal Clean Air Act?

After being home on vacation for a couple of weeks, I know what my neighbor means when he comes over to our house and wants to know, "Where is that little stinker?"

Despite all of this, I'm not discouraged. There are still a couple of things we can try. Moonbeam thinks we should make Maggie sit with her head out the window as long as it is downwind. Sadistic Daughter is trying to teach Maggie to hold her breath when she is in the house. Our other daughter suggested we all wear surgical masks.

Putting all of the above aside, I'm trying to look at the bright side. Maggie does make a good watchdog. If someone tried to break in, they would immediately turn back. Why? Because they would take one sniff and recognize this house is already the scene of a crime.

> " 'What's your sign?' I said. She held up a stop sign."
> Henny Youngman

Moonbeam has been on an astrology kick the last couple of weeks. She was reading a book the other day and informed me that she is a Sagittarius and I'm an Aries. I don't know what that means but, she announced that, according to our astrological charts, we are exact opposites. I don't need an astrological chart to tell me that. I picked up on that fact the first time I saw her in

In China It's The Year Of The Septic Tank

a sweater.

She gave me a little book that's supposed to contain my astrological forecast for the entire year. Skeptic that I am, I compared what the book said was going to happen during the previous month with what actually happened. According to my astrological forecast, I was supposed to get an increase in salary sometime between the 5th and the 8th. Since that did not happen, I showed the book to my boss and asked him if he had overlooked something. He laughed. Then he said that astrological forecasts weren't running the business. That's when I told him I couldn't find his sign anywhere in the book. I think he's a "Miser." Misers and Aries are opposites too.

In some cases this astrological book Moonbeam gave me turned out to be fairly accurate. On the 27th I was supposed to meet someone new and exciting. That part of my forecast came true. I backed into some woman's car at the Dairy Queen. Sure enough ... I didn't know her and I can assure you, both she and her husband were definitely excited. The thing that disappoints me is my astrological forecast didn't say anything about the size of her husband and his propensity to render bodily harm. Let me put it like this, since that little fender bending incident in the DQ parking lot, a while new picture comes to mind when I hear the word "excited."

On the 30th I was supposed to hear from a distant relative. I did. Our son called from California; he wanted us to send him money. I asked him what for and he said a new surfboard. He's supposed to be studying for the real estate boards.

On the 13th of the following month I was supposed to have an encounter with an old acquaintance. The guy who prepared my astrological forecast must have had a sense of humor. That was the day I had to go in for an income tax audit. The IRS lady was the one I ran into at the Dairy Queen.

So much for my checkered past.

The Curmudgeon Rides Again

I decided to sneak a peek at the upcoming months to see if I would fare any better. You may be interested to know that when I study my astrological forecast, I feel a lot is left to interpretation. For example, the stars indicate that I can expect to move into a "bigger house." My accountant says that if I didn't start keeping better tax records, that "bigger house" could be the federal prison.

In truth though, I became so intrigued with this horriblescope business that I purchased a copy of an Oriental astrological guide. Their system is different than ours. Instead of being confined to one period during the course of the year ... they give you a whole year. I just happen to have been born into the year of the Dog. It could have been the year of the Rat, the Tiger, the Horse, the Goat, or several other equally unappealing others. I asked Moonbeam what Oriental sign she thought I was born under. She guessed the year of the Snake. If not the Snake, she said, then it would probably be the Monkey or the Rat. When I told her it was none of those she said I had reminded her why she didn't put much credence in the Oriental astrological forecast.

Actually, being born in the year of the Dog isn't so bad. I'm in there with such other notables as Adolph Hitler, the Boston Strangler, Lee Harvey Oswald, and the shark from *Jaws*. I look at it this way, at least folks have heard of some of the folks born under my sign.

It's kind of interesting to see who is born under other Oriental signs. For example, movie star Tom Selleck was born in the year of the Rooster. Mick Jagger, the Rock star, was born in the year of the Goat and Cary Grant was born under the sign of the Rabbit. Jackie Kennedy Onassis was born in the year of the Snake and Marilyn Monroe was born in the year of the Tiger. Interesting?

I told my boss that I had learned he was born in the same Oriental year as former President Ronald Reagan and Vice President Dan Quayle. Boy, oh boy, was he proud. I can't wait to drop the other shoe. That's when I tell him that was the year of the Pig.

"What do you send a sick florist?" Henny Youngman

(The scene is the CNN television studios in New York. Larry King is interviewing Doctor Henry Frankenstein, creator of the famous Frankenstein monster.)

L.K. "Good evening, Doctor Frankenstein, and welcome to our show."

H.F. "Vas is goot to be here, Harry."

L.K. "That's Larry, Doctor."

H.F. "Larry, Berry, Harry, Cary, vot difference does it make? Vee all end up da same vay some day."

L.K. "That's very interesting, Doctor. I suppose that's the philosophy that led you to create your monster."

H.F. "You heard about dat, huh? Vat a boo boo I make. He vas von ugly dude, vasn't he? But it vasn't my fault you know."

L.K. "You say it wasn't your fault."

H.F. "Of course not. It vas dat stupo, Igor. Vat a dumbo! 'Get me da brain of a smarty type,' I tell him. But vat does he do? He gets me da brain of a politician. Believe me, Mr. King, I vould not have put such a brain in such a big type guy if I had known. Very dangerous combination, brute power and a politician's mentality."

L.K. "Well, Doctor, if you felt your assistant was so incompetent, why didn't you replace him? Perhaps this whole unfortunate incident with the monster could have been avoided."

H.F. "Vell dere is no question vhat if I had it to do over again I vould do it different."

L.K. "Like starting with a new assistant, I suppose?"

H.F. "Yah, den I vould get Vanna Vhite to be my assistant."

L.K. "Vanna White? Interesting choice. I didn't know she had any medical training."

H.F. "Who cares vhat kind of training she got. Tink about it. Me and Vanna alone in dat, dark, lonely, scary, castle mit da thunderboomers and lightning crashing all around. Now dats da kind of assistant a mad doctor should have ... not like dat ugly stupo, Igor."

L.K. "That's an interesting term you used, Doctor. You used the term 'mad doctor.' Is that the way you think of your self ... a 'mad doctor?'"

H.F. "Vell to tell da trooth, Larry, I'm not real mad, just kinda vhat you Americans call 'ticked off.'"

L.K. "Let's get back to what you would do differently if you had it all to do over again."

H.F. "Vell, da first ting I vould do is get me von of dem Acme New Body Parts kits, none of dis putting together a bunch of used body parts. Dey make neat vons in California, you know. Lots of silicone and stuff. Maybe den I vould come up with something like Tina Turner or Sharon Stone. Who vould call me mad den? Finally I vould get me a real high class brain ... from von of dem corporate types."

L.K. "You mean the brain of a corporate executive?"

H.F. "Vhat is dis mit you interviewer types always repeating vhat somebody said? Yah, I vant a corporate executive type brain; dat vay I get blind obedience ... nothing original, no questioning, dey just do vhat I tell dem to do. Dey

	are trained dat vay you know."
L.K.	"What else?"
H.F.	"I tink maybe I make my next monster more like Elvis. Know vhat I mean? Lots of moving around, bumping, grinding. You know, monster appeal. Dat is pretty frightening, no? I mean vat vas dis clomp-clomp-clomp stuff my first monster did vhen he vas valking around. No rhythm. No vonder people didn't like him."
L.K.	"What other changes would you make?"
H.F.	"I'd get him a job vhere he could mumble and grunt and make lots of money ... like von of dose announcers on MTV. But none of dis is going to happen you know. I'm stuck with Igor as my stupo assistant."
L.K.	"And why is that, Doctor?"
H.F.	"The stupo is my wife's cousin."

"I never had a penny to my name, so I changed my name."
Henny Youngman

Have you ever had a bad hair day?

I have. In fact, I've had bad hair days that lasted for years. When I look back and think about it, most of my life has been a bad hair day.

When I started high school I had what folks in those days call a *butch cut*. A *butch cut* is like a *buzz cut* except a *buzz cut* (excuse the expression) is a hair shorter than a *butch*. I never have been real savvy when it came to telling the barber how I wanted my hair cut ... and it has taken a long time to get this hair thing straightened out.

Let's start with the fact that there are two varieties of the *butch* haircut, namely the *crew cut* and the *flat top*. This caused me no end of consternation. All the football players wore *crew cuts*. All the guys that hung out at Walgreen's drug store down on Calhoun Street wore *flat tops*. The biggest difference I could see (beside the hair) was the football players all limped a lot and the guys that hung out at Walgreen's were the ones that got all the dates and went to all the dances.

It's easy to see why this was a period of indecision in my life. I couldn't make up my mind whether I wanted to have a *crew cut*, get my nose broken and be a football player – or if I wanted to hang out at Walgreen's and maybe someday meet a girl.

What did I do? I hung out at Walgreen's for two years, had a cool *flat top* all that time and never could get a date. So I changed my approach. My buddy, Sebenoler, told me I needed to make some changes. So I decided to do what any self-respecting, overweight high school junior with terminal acne would do ... I denounced women, dedicated my life to football and got a *butch* haircut. I also got a broken nose and broke my leg. Guys who breathe thru their mouth and walk around on crutches don't get many dates either.

After high school came the Air Force. The summer I graduated from high school and before going into the service, I let my hair grow and wore it in something called a *pompadour*. A *pompadour* makes a guy look like he has a growth on his forehead just above the hairline and all that hair is trying to hide the fact. When a guy has a double chin and a *pompadour*, he tends to look like he has lumps on both the top and bottom of his head. Before the Air Force would take me, it wanted to know if there was something on my head I was trying to hide. Actually, I didn't have to give my hair much thought while I was in the Air Force. They had pretty well thought the matter through for me.

Hair wasn't an issue again until I got out of the service and headed off to college. The first thing I learned was no one cared how you got your hair cut in college. When I was in college there was the *hippie* cut, the *bowl* cut, the *hockey* cut, and the *Red Sea* cut. The *hippie* cut wasn't really a haircut, it was a happening. I tried it once and someone told me I looked like a Brillo pad with ears. It didn't take me long to figure out that the *bowl* cut (same length all the way around) and the *hockey* cut (parted in the middle and worn down over the ears) wasn't for me either. For awhile the *Red Sea* cut intrigued me, but I could never get my hair parted both in the middle and in a straight line at the same time. On me it looked like the *Dead Sea* cut.

When I finally graduated from college I was confronted with the hair issue all over again. Among my choices were the *slick-back* cut, the *businessman's* cut, and the *professional* cut. I walked into the barbershop and told the barber I wanted a *professional* cut (parted on the side and somewhat longer than the *businessman's* cut).

"What do you do for a living?" the barber wanted to know.

"Just out of college and looking for a job," I admitted.

"Then you can't have a *professional* haircut until you have a profession," he said.

"Then how about a *businessman's* cut?" I asked.

"Not until you are one," he said.

"All right, give me a *slick back* cut," I decided.

The barber gave me a long, fatherly look and said, "Son, don't you realize that if you wear your hair in a *slick back* cut, no one will hire you?"

Well, all of that was a long time ago.

Kinda sad isn't it? Now, years later, looking back on my mediocre achievements, I guess I can blame my lack of success on the fact I just never could get the right haircut.

"When you're down and out, lift up your head & shout, 'Help!'"
Henny Youngman

There was one of those thought-provoking articles in the newspaper the other day. A researcher in Texas published the results of his year-long study that indicated workers who were supervised by a woman were happier than those who were supervised by a man. The moment I read it, bells started going off and I thought to myself, *flawed study*. On the other hand, if I worked for Sharon Stone, I'd show you one ecstatic employee.

But you know me, I'm picky, a real doubter. Curmudgeons are supposed to be that way. After digesting this particular article, I came to the conclusion there are a few chinks in this report. In other words, it invites challenge. Nowhere, for example, in any of the data presented in this article does it say what kind of bosses and what kinds of occupations were surveyed. By that I mean I could find nothing in the article that indicated this researcher wasn't just rehashing the age-old question of who is better at motivating people, men or women. That's objection number one.

Second objection, never did our erstwhile purveyor of new knowledge mention the number of people in his study. He deals entirely with percentages, which leads me to believe I am perfectly justified (during my stinging rebuttal) in being allowed to make my point in the same fashion.

To get to the truth of the matter of who makes a superior boss, I asked two members of my poker club whether it was better to work for a man or a woman. Barney Fritt said he would have to vote for a man. Barney is a bachelor and a plumber. He says his father is the only one he ever worked for because his dad owns the plumbing business and none of the other plumbing firms in town would hire him. Regardless of Barney's background, he is employed and he did indicate his preference for a man boss.

Jake Thump was the other worker in my survey and he said he wasn't sure who would make a better boss. He did say he would like some clarification on just exactly what I meant by "boss." Unfortunately, it didn't do much good to explain the term "boss" to Jake because he was equally confused by the terms "job" and "paycheck."

All that notwithstanding, there is no disputing my findings. The results of my survey were diametrically opposed to the findings of the gentleman from Texas. In my survey, 50 % of the men surveyed thought a "male" boss would be better.

It also occurred to me (as I'm certain it did you) that the kind of job the employee had to do would have a bearing on whether or not a man or woman would make a better boss. To prove my point I asked my two survey participants this question. "Who would make a better boss if your job was skinning muskrats?"

Barney thought, although he admitted he did not have any experience with such an occupation, that a man would make a better boss supervising a bunch of muskrat skinners. Jake wanted to know what a muskrat was. But, once again, 50% of the participants in my survey thought a man would be a better boss.

At this point I think you can begin to see why I doubted the veracity of the Texas report. But for those of you who feel I still haven't proved my point, there is more.

To give weight to my findings, I expanded my survey to include two additional members of my poker club when they returned from watching the mud wrestling special on television. This time I asked my four male survey participants whether they thought compassion, sympathy, tenderness, gentleness, benevolence, understanding and tolerance were important characteristics for a boss.

The terms confused them. Barney proved the point by saying that no one in the survey could think of a boss that exhibited any of those "sissy" tendencies.

We can conclude from that, of course, that since men have been getting the job done (this is not a debate, this is a survey) for many years now, the attributes listed above are both unimportant and unnecessary in a boss. In other words, 100% of the men surveyed felt that evidence of the milk of human kindness in a boss was totally unnecessary.

Finally, I posed this question to my poker buddies. "Can you think of any reason why a woman would make a better boss than a man?"

Frank Twirpy thought at length before he answered. "If she was good lookin' it would help. The guy I work for looks and smells like an opossum, so I guess anyone would be an improvement."

It took Jake Thump to put it into perspective though. "If you ask me," Jake muttered, " ... any guy that thinks he's the boss, good or bad, is just kiddin' himself. Sooner or later even my boss has got to go home to his wife. I figure that's when he learns who is really runnin' the show."

"Then you guys really think that the women are boss," I said.

"We don't think it; we know it," Jake acknowledged.

After listening to these guys respond to my questions, I think I'll look for a new poker club.

"My wife missed her nap today ... she slept right through it."
Henny Youngman

Five, maybe six years ago (it's probably a good thing that no one remembers exactly) the youngest of our three sons came home from college at Christmas with a sad story. The scenario involved howling winds, bitter temperatures and a homeless puppy.

Now you need to know that Kendrick, or Studly, as we affectionately refer to number three son, just may be one of the world's great manipulators. That particular night he concluded his saga of sadness by making one of those statements designed to turn a paternal heart to butter. "I know how you love dogs, Dad, and I knew you wouldn't mind if I brought her home over Christmas."

Bait taken. Hook swallowed. But for some and obviously now not recalled reason, I interpreted my son's remark to mean that when Studly returned to campus, he was taking that cute little ball of black fur with him.

Wrong. Signal misinterpreted. *Cute Little Puppy* (that was her name then) had moved in ... apparently for good.

Well, as you know, time has a way of passing and puppies have a way of growing. *CLP* (Cute Little Puppy), now known as *Freight Train*, has increased in height and girth and has learned several tricks, most of which she taught herself.

Trick number one is called eating. Freight Train is very good at eating. She can inhale more Purina Dog Chow in one snarf than many dogs do in a lifetime. The problem is ... this thing with eating is a double-edged sword; it's not only how much she eats but when she eats. Somewhere along the line, Freight Train has decided that night time is chow time. Many is the night I have laid there listening to her chomp chow.

Trick number two in the repertoire is called "drinking water in a loud and obnoxious fashion." It's a scientific fact, Freight Train can drink more water in one sitting than any ten men toiling on the Alaskan pipe line.

Trick number three has to do with the way Freight Train leaves her footprints around the house. Actually, I disagree with Moonbeam on this one; I don't think this has anything to do with her enormous weight. The problem is she has feet the size of dinner plates. Because of this, Freight Train no longer has access to the entire house ... only my studio. For some time now I've been thinking about turning my studio over to her and moving into her doghouse. Hey, she doesn't use her doghouse, and if I did move in I'd have more room.

Trick number four consists of barking at everything that goes bump in the night. For awhile it was enough to put her out on the back deck when the moon came out, but that ended when she woke me up several nights in a row chasing the raccoons off the deck. In all honesty though, I can see her point. Raccoons haven't any business on our back deck.

Trick number five I blame on the fact that Freight Train is a bit on the exuberant side. She has never learned to walk; she bounces or runs everywhere she goes. At 80 pounds that's a lot of bouncing. When she roars down the stairs to go out for our morning walk, everything in Moonbeam's china closet rattles around and does a little dance. This tends to irritate my bride but I think it's kinda cool. I think it sounds like windchimes.

Trick number six is Freight Train's imitation of Moonbeam's Uncle Ralph. I'm trying to think of a discreet (or at least, socially acceptable) way of describing the phenomena in question. Let me put it like this ... it's sorta like that thing that happens to most of us after a ham and bean supper at the church.

I know what you're thinking, six tricks isn't all that many.

Well, there's a reason for that; Freight Train is only 10 months old. She'll probably live to be 14 or 15 years old. There's plenty of time for her to learn more tricks.

Wait a minute. I just heard the door slam. I think that was Moonbeam leaving.

"Walk into an antique store sometime and say, 'What's new?'"
Henny Youngman

A couple of weeks ago I passed along the Curmudgeon's observations on rhetorical questions. A week or so later a reader sent me a note and said he wasn't sure he understood the difference between an ordinary question and a rhetorical question. Let me answer it this way. A rhetorical question is one which the person asking the question is unlikely to receive an answer. For example, "How high is up?" is a rhetorical question. The question is intended to spur one's thinking only. No answer is expected. However, when a father asks a young man what the lad's intentions are toward his daughter, that is not a rhetorical question. He expects an answer ... and it better be the right one.

I first learned about rhetorical questions in high school when Sister Malice used to confront me with a series of rhetorical questions several times a week. I knew that they were rhetorical questions because I never knew the answer to any of them.

At any rate, that column on RQs a couple of weeks back triggered a number of phone calls, several pieces of mail and a number of reader offerings. So much for background.

A woman from Coldwater (under most circumstances I would have used the term *lady*, but I got in trouble with the people who run the *Fort Wayne New Sentinel* who said the term was sexist), sent me the following RQs.

"Tell me how they get the deer to cross the highway where they post those yellow *deer crossing* signs."

Or how about coming up with an answer for this. 'Why is the word abbreviation such a long word?"

How about this one. It comes from an inmate at Jackson State Prison. He wants to know why they sterilize needles when they give lethal injections.

A Steuben County resident wants to know if it is true that cannibals won't eat clowns because they taste funny.

That last RQ reminds me of a section in one of Phyllis Diller's books (remember her?) titled *Phyllis Diller's Most Successful Recipes*. The pages were blank. Miss Diller is the same one who believed it was unwise to tell her friends that she would be doing the cooking for her upcoming dinner party because no one would come.

One of my friends at Tri State wanted to know why they call it a TV set when you only get one at a time.

Moonbeam's Uncle Ralph (this one is really intriguing because I did not realize he could read) asked, "If you choke a Smurf, what color does it turn?" I showed this question to Moonbeam in an attempt to prove my contention that her Uncle Ralph, despite his years, still hasn't progressed past the comic pages.

My bride had this contribution. She wants to know why there is an expiration date on sour cream containers. This reminds me of one of Hoosier philosopher Abe Martin's more quotable quotes. "The husband who never complains about what his wife sets in front of him at the dinner table may live somewhat more peacefully, but certainly not as long."

Abe Martin is also the one who said, "Very often the quiet feller is the one who has told you all he knows."

In China It's The Year Of The Septic Tank

Back to the RQs. Have you got an answer for this one? "If corn oil comes from corn, where does baby oil come from?" That one goes right along with the question, "If vegetarians eat vegetables, then what do humanitarians eat?"

Hey, you English buffs, how about this one. "What's another word for thesaurus?"

Marian Franklin, a writer from Fort Wayne wants to know if *fuzzy logic* tickles.

This one comes from one of the guys in my poker club. He's the one who is always complaining about all the noise made on his lake by personal watercraft. "If it's tourist season," he wants to know, "can we shoot 'em?"

Matt Clemens of Davenport, Iowa (another writer friend) wants to know if radioactive cats have 18 half-lives. He is the same one who asks the penetrating question: "If you are driving along and you throw your cat out of the car window, does it become kitty litter?"

Are you hooked? Want some more?

"What was the best thing before sliced bread?"

"How does a Scotsman know when it's time to tune his bagpipes?"

"What do they use to ship Styrofoam?"

"How old is dirt?"

"If Jesus had a brother, what would his name be?"

Okay, that's enough. But, if, by any chance you didn't happen to know the answer to one or two of these little gems, ask a teenager. They know everything.

The Curmudgeon Rides Again

"Things were rough when I was a baby. No talcum powder."
Henny Youngman

I hate ties.

Ties are void of any redeeming value.

Women, who are a lot smarter than men, gave up their girdles a long time ago. Unfortunately, men are slower to catch on. Hey, for any of you guys out there who happen to be reading this, the dark ages are over, ties are no longer in vogue. No matter what your wife, your boss, or your minister tells you, they just aren't necessary.

Ties are obsolete.

Not very many men know this but ties were invented by women. Ties are an integral part of the universal sisterhood's Machiavellian plan to get even with men. What are they getting even for? Take your pick. Child birth, pantyhose, who knows?

My mother used to make me wear a tie to church. Every Sunday morning she would loop that sucker around my neck a couple of times and finish it off with a big old Windsor knot. She wasn't satisfied until my cheeks had a warm, pinkish glow. The glow, of course, had nothing to do with the state of my health; the tie was too tight.

What's wrong with ties? To start with, ties cost too much. Worse, no matter how many ties a guy has in his closet, he never has the right one. First of all, there are too many different styles (wide, narrow, bow, clip-on, string) made out of too many different fabrics (silk, rayon, polyester, coarse hemp and sack cloth) in too many colors ranging from puce to chartreuse. Even if there was only one style in one color made out of one fabric ... it would be one too many.

In China It's The Year Of The Septic Tank

The day I burned most of my ties, I had ties with school emblems, the company logo, product names, designer's names, and one with an obscene social comment. I still have ties that I haven't worn in ten years and can't throw them away. Why? Because I can't remember who gave them to me. A sure-fire formula for hurt feelings in our loving domicile involves one of my clumsy attempts to dispose of one of these paisley or checkered artifacts of a by-gone day. Every time I do, it elicits a comment that goes something like, "Don't you like the ties I pick out?" That question of course uttered by Moonbeam as liquid pools form in her lovely brown orbs.

"It's stained," I lie.

"I'll get it cleaned," she says helpfully. All the while I'm shaking my head ... knowing full well that if I let that happen I'll have another five bucks invested in something that will hang in my closet for another ten years.

For a while the territorial approach worked. On those occasions when I received a tie or dress shirt I didn't like, I would hurry down to the Elks and drag it through the chicken gravy on the steam table. That way I didn't have to prove I liked it and I didn't have to worry about wearing it because it had something spilled on it. It was branded and everyone believed I liked it. Everyone thinks chicken gravy stains are an indication I really like something.

When you think about it, ties make about as much sense as taking out collision insurance on a super modified out at Dick Poe's Angola Speedway. The three people who gave me ties last Christmas are on my hit list.

One of my Christmas ties is painted to look like a fish. It's made of silk. Who ever heard of a silk fish? Who hangs a silk fish around their neck? Could you wear a tie to work that was painted to look like a carp? Maybe I could wear it to church the Sunday

The Curmudgeon Rides Again

we get our annual seven loaves and two fishes sermon. That would sorta be appropriate. Pastor Good would look out at the congregation, spot that carp tie I was wearing, and think it was a "sign" for certain.

Sadistic Daughter gave me a tie too. She knows better. It's red and black. You know, a checkerboard design. When I put it on I look like a box of Purina Cat Chow.

One of my co-workers gave me a tie once. It had a naughty word cleverly woven into the fabric. I didn't catch it. I wore it to work and our secretary's face turned red. The waitress at lunch gave me a dirty look and a fat lady at the supermarket punched me out. "That's disgusting," she said, and marched off to complain to the store manager. He asked me not to come back until I could act like a gentleman. I'll bet most of you guys out there never realized a tie could get you in trouble.

Men of America, arise! Throw off the shackles of convention. Someday this week go to work without a tie. Then, after we succeed in getting our bosses and wives used to the idea of not wearing a tie, we'll tackle another stupid and completely pointless travesty against the brotherhood. Shaving.

My Wife Drives A Momserati

As I write this, this august household has two drivers and three cars. We also have a son who is hooked on and collects Maseratis. You need to know this to understand the saga I am about to unfold.

Several years ago my brother-in-law, weary of paying for car insurance and license fees on a car he did not use, decided to sell the no-longer-useful vehicle.

Hardly worth mentioning you say?

It happens all the time you say?

Before you go on to other things, perhaps I need to mention that the vehicle in question was a 1981 Dodge Aries. Pallid yellow in color from years of sitting in the hot summer sun, headliner sagging, sporting numerous but superficial rust spots; it was made available to my wife for the paltry sum of one dollar.

Overall I would rate the condition of the car at the time of purchase as "sorry." Windows would not roll down (rust). Doors protested mightily when faced with the awesome task of opening and closing (oil). Engine performance can best be described with terms such as inferior, inadequate, and cheesy.

Did this discourage my soulmate? Negative, no way, nay, and no siree. In her mind the 1981 Aries K was worth saving. Why? Because even though it was close to 19 years old, it only had 23,000 miles on it. Why would a car of that vintage have so few miles on it you ask? Because, my sister-in-law refused to ride in it. The sorry beast did not have air conditioning.

When my bride of forty odd years took it to her favorite automotive repairman, he took one look at what she was driving and began smiling. He doubtless figured it was no longer necessary to invest in the market; he had discovered a sure-fire annuity. By the time he got the Momserati up and running, he figured he would be financially secure for life.

Is it necessary to tell you that repair bills on the Momserati soon became more frequent and costly than maintaining a teenage girl in the style to which she believes she is entitled? As I recall, there was even a discussion or two as to whether or not it made fiscal sense to purchase a Chrysler agency in order to reduce the cost of repairs.

Eventually though, my bride and the Momserati reached what can best be described as an understanding. The beast would cooperate as long as Madam School Nurse was driving, not her husband. If, by some terrible and perverse twist of fate, I was forced to drive the car (brute, yahoo, chariot of the Goths), automotive difficulties would soon surface.

Momserati stalled at the bank and would not start. Momserati stalled at the theater and would not start. One time Momserati started and would not stop (not brakes ... the engine). How did I solve that problem? I considered driving it into the lake and telling my bride "her car had drowned." Instead I resorted to stopping my bride's chariot of grief and yanking out every wire that looked like it might contribute to engine performance. You should have seen Car Repairman grin when I brought the beast in for that particular round of repairs.

My Wife Drives A Momserati

Recently I told my bride that in my opinion ("opinion" being the operative word here), she should get rid of her Momserati. But you know what they say about opinions ... "Opinions are like _ _ _ _ _ _ _ _, everyone has one." (Have fun filling in the blank.)

The Curmudgeon Rides Again

"It ain't a fit night out for man nor beast."
W.C. Fields
The Fatal Glass of Beer, 1933

I'll let you in on a secret. Writers like rain. They also, if they are really serious about their writing, like snow, fog, and those wonderful dark and dreary days we get from time to time.

Why is that? Bad weather is good writing weather. No one likes to sit inside at their computer or word processor on a nice sunny day. Writers get the feeling they are missing out on something when they have to work on a sunny day. This fact alone should prove that writers aren't as different from other people as most folks think they are.

The bottom line is this. If I have a lot of writing to do, I do not want it to be a nice, cheerful day. Sometimes, when I'm working on a really long piece of writing, I'll pray for several dismal days in a row. I don't often get the somber or rainy weather rain I'm praying for though. This makes me think the reason I don't get the uninviting weather I want is for one or more of the following reasons:

    A.   God is not a writer. He doesn't see the need for forlorn weather. I look at it this way, if he enjoyed writing he probably wouldn't have had other people write the Bible. He'd have done it himself.

    B.   The folks who don't want rain are praying a whole lot harder than the folks who do want rain.

    C.   "Rain wanters" are outnumbered by the "rain don't wanters." This is probably one of those most good for the most people issues.

While I'm at it though, I might as well get really curmudgeonly and mention some of my other dislikes. Take those forms you get in the mail for instance. They ask you to sign your name at the bottom if everything you wrote on the form is true. When they do that I'm tempted to write, "I won't sign my name to this because one of the statements I made on this form is an untruth." Then, out in the margin I write, "If you can figure out which statement is an untruth, send it back and I'll sign it." They never do.

I also dislike secretaries who say, "May I ask what this call is in reference to?" when I call their boss. I know their boss probably tells them to say that because he or she doesn't like surprises. But I don't like to have to repeat things twice either. One time a secretary asked me that and I told her I was the employment agency that had been hired to find him a new secretary. I wasn't, of course, but I'll bet he had a hard time explaining that one.

One of the things I don't like most is the middle seat of an airplane. There are a lot of reasons why this is one of my dislikes. First of all, I feel like a piece of lunch meat when I sit wedged in between two other people. Second, I paid as much money to ride that airplane as everyone else. Why don't I get a window or an aisle seat? If I sit in a window seat I can see out. I like to make certain the engine on my side of the plane is working. If I sit in an aisle seat it's easier for me to get to the restroom. It's a hassle making someone get up so I can go to the restroom.

Another pet peeve of mine is long legged valets/parking attendants who bring your car back to you after the concert and don't bother to put your seat back up where it belongs. I get in and I can't reach the pedals. Sometimes I can't even reach the steering wheel. By the time I get all the buttons, levers, and such adjusted, the guy in the car behind me is leaning on his horn telling me to get moving. There are times when I'm tempted to get out of my car and walk back to the car making all the noise to tell him I can't help it if I have short legs.

Another thing. People who say, "Have a nice day," disturb me. The church I was raised in teaches their members to feel guilty about almost everything. Having a nice day makes me feel guilty. I think it's because I don't think I deserve a nice day. All of which may be at the root of me wanting bad weather so I can feel good about writing.

But, if I got the bad weather I was praying for, I would have to feel guilty about that. Why? Because I wouldn't think I deserved it. But it could be because God had started writing his own material.

"How old would you be if you didn't know how old you was?"
Satchel Paige
New York Times
June 8, 1984

I've come to the conclusion that the reason I'm starting to forget things cannot be blamed on my age. The reason I can't remember things is because I've already got too much stuff in my brain. It's not necessarily good stuff. It's just, well ... stuff.

Recently I've started taking inventory of things in my brain that I don't use anymore. I'm doing this because I think if I do a little spring brain cleaning, I may have some room for some of the things I'm supposed to remember. In a computer, that's called storage capacity. It isn't so much that I need an upgrade, I've got to find my delete button.

There are lots of things up there (I'm referring to my brain – at least I hope it's still up there) that are useless. For example, there is my military service number. That was a long time ago but

I still remember it. How many times does someone ask me what my service number was during the course of the year? Not very often. I'm too old to go back in the Air Force. Nevertheless, there those eight digits are ... just waiting to work their way into the conversation.

Numbers seem to be cluttering up a lot of my recall capacity. For example, I remember my boss's telephone number from back in my "real job" days. That's real mind clutter. Not only am I trying to forget my boss's telephone number, I'm trying to forget my boss as well.

To show you what I mean about numbers getting in the way of a person's remembering capacity, think about your social security number. That's an even bigger number than the military service number (nine digits compared to eight), but there it is right on the tip of my tongue when someone wants to know what my social security number is. Why should that be? The government gives us a card with our social security number on it when we're just getting started. If all you have to do is look in your billfold to see what your social security number is, why go to all the trouble of remembering it? Think what you could do with the space those nine digits take up.

Part of the problem is I remember dumb and useless numbers. I don't remember numbers that would make my life a little easier. People always want to know what your license number is when you check into a hotel or motel. I can't remember license numbers. Sometimes I can't even remember what car I'm driving. If I am lucky enough to remember the car, I have to go outside and look at the license plate in order to fill out that little card when you register at the place you are going to sleep that night.

Sometimes I have trouble remembering numbers that are said to be for our convenience. Someone is always asking me what my telephone number is. I don't know what it is because I seldom use it. When someone asks me where I live, I don't tell them the number. I tell them such and such a house from the corner or some landmark. If I'm telling a man where I live I reference how far it is from the tavern. If it's a woman I'm giving directions, I tell them what direction and how far it is from the shopping center. They can always figure it out if I reference the shopping center.

Some people are like me; they have too much stuff up there to remember a lot of numbers like in an address. Women can tell you how much so and so paid for a dress, but they have a lot of trouble remembering to tell their husbands how much they paid. Men can never remember how much they lost at the Tuesday night poker club. That's because they are still fuming over the amount they lost the last time they played. I contend we all need more remembering space.

In the old days, a person didn't have to be a numbers remembering machine. Now though, our nation has gone numbers crazy. Street address, office telephone, home telephone, fax number, cell phone number, checking account numbers (hard to remember because the numbers on the checks are printed funny), various credit card numbers and a whole lot more I've probably forgotten. How many times have you called the bank and the first thing they say is, "May I have your account number, please?"

See what I mean? If I could get rid of all these useless numbers rattling around in my head, I'd probably be a better person. I might even remember our anniversary.

> "If a man is a fool, the best thing to do to get him to advertise that fact, is let him speak aloud."
> Woodrow Wilson
> Paris, May 10, 1919

My wife is one of those home-spun folks who likes to use famous quotations, allusions, and passages to prove her point. For example, she might say something like, "Save your money for a rainy day." You've heard people say that. In another time and under other circumstances, she might say, "The more the merrier." You probably heard that one too.

Okay, by now you're saying, "What's your point?" (People say that a lot when they talk to me.)

My point is, I don't happen to agree with some of these sayings. Take the "save your money for a rainy day" piece of advice. I think that's all wet. Some people, like writers and farmers, like rainy days. That doesn't mean we are going out there and spend some of our saved money just because it's raining. Think about it. What do you do on a rainy day? Most folks sit around and grumble about the weather when it rains. They don't go shopping because they are going to get wet going from their car to where ever it is they are going. My point is most folks don't go out and spend money when it rains. They stay at home and wish it wasn't raining.

I think it makes more sense to save your money for a beautiful day. Then you can go out and enjoy it.

Then there is that old "the more the merrier" bit. Not so. This is another fallacy. The slogan "the more the merrier" was probably developed by bus people or cruise ship directors. If

The Curmudgeon Rides Again

there are a whole bunch of people it's hard to get a table at a restaurant. If you take a trip with lots of people you probably won't get a good seat on the bus. Either that or you'll end up sitting next to someone who chews with their mouth open or never stops talking.

If you think about it, "... the fewer, the merrier" makes a whole lot more sense. Every time I go with a bunch of people to something it turns out to be a disaster. One time I went to a football game with a bunch of guys. The people who sponsored the trip provided us with beer and sandwiches. The guys started drinking beer when we left the city limits. Ten minutes hadn't passed when they started insisting that the driver stop at every rest stop. I'll bet if we hadn't run out of beer we wouldn't have made it to the game.

Moonbeam has never said, "Rise and shine," but my mother did. I'm not certain this is good advice, especially if you went to bed late. Then it's likely to be "Rise and wish you hadn't." Back in the days when we had lots of horses I used to get up early. I'd feed horses, take a shower, jump in my pickup and head for town to get "in town" chores done. But, stores weren't open so I'd go for coffee. Waitresses, who had to get up even earlier than I did, were surly, and none of my coffee-drinking friends were there yet.

I say it should go something like, "Rise and hope the world hasn't gone down the drain while you were asleep."

How about that old saying, "Early to bed, early to rise, makes a man healthy, wealthy, and wise"?

There are any number of holes in this one. First of all, it says "men" ... I want to know what it does for women? And, how exactly is it going to make me wise? Then I want to know who made up this less-than-intelligent-saying to start with? It may be a cute little jingle but there sure are a lot of places where it leads you astray. If you go to bed early you miss the ten o'clock news. Then you lay there and worry something may have happened that you should know about. It's not easy to sleep when you are worried. If you get up early, there is no one to talk to. I think the really "wise" people are getting a little extra sleep. "Early to bed, etc." might make you sound like a discerning thinker but it just doesn't hold water.

Another one that doesn't make sense is, "Save your pennies." Do you know how many pennies you have to save before they amount to something? I saved pennies for years. Then I took them to the bank. They were really heavy. The bank gave me thirty-seven dollars and fourteen cents for my effort. It cost more than that to have the hernia repaired.

Saint: (noun) A dead sinner revised and edited.
Ambrose Bierce
The Devil's Dictionary
1906

I was reading an article about saints the other day. Not the New Orleans Saints. Not Saint Bernards. I'm talking about the other kind of Saints, as the article put it, "Once-ordinary people who brought a holy purpose to every task and thereby might inspire us moderns." (I think when the article used the term "moderns" it was referring to anyone with a social security number, indoor plumbing, or the Internet.)

A couple of things both intrigued and surprised me about this article. First of all, it seems the church has added quite a number of Saints to the list since my Saint studying days. Back when I was a pup there were only a handful of Saints. It was

The Curmudgeon Rides Again

pretty tough to gain admittance to the Saint's Club.

According to this article though, admission requirements appear to have loosened up in the Saint's Club. My hunch is there may be a new admissions director up there. Maybe the former one retired. He had to be getting up in years ... at least five or six thousand years old.

Did you happen to notice I used the term "up there?" That's another assumption on my part ... that Saints go "up there." That's probably a bad assumption. I don't think Saints would be very useful "up there." Most of the problems seem to be "down here."

My favorite Saint of all time is Saint Francis. Saint Francis was cool. Saint Francis is the Patron Saint of animals. Every time you see a statue of him he has a bird sitting on his shoulder. That isn't what the birds do to me.

According to this article, people like Saint John Baptist de la Salle and Saint Martin de Porres are now Saints. Saint John Baptist de la Salle is reported to be the Patron Saint of teachers. Teachers? I have to be honest with you, I didn't know teachers had a Patron Saint. I don't think any of my teachers did. Of course most of them were nuns and I always believed their right to crack me across the knuckles with that walnut pointer they carried around came straight from a higher authority than your everyday, run of the mill Saint.

Saint Therese of Lisieux is the Patron Saint of airline pilots. But the passengers who fly on those airlines depend on Saint Joseph of Cupertino. The only Cupertino I know is in California. According to what I read, Saint Joseph of Cupertino could levitate. Not everyone can do that. Our oldest son lives in California. I'm going to ask him if he has seen anyone around Cupertino levitating.

Did you know there was a Patron Saint of music? Her name is Saint Cecillia. If she includes rock musicians in her coverage, she is probably tone deaf and sings flat.

According to the Paul II Culture Center in Washington, D.C. there are 1,474 Saints and 568 "Blesseds." Blesseds are people who are on the waiting list for canonization. You can check all this out at *e3mil.com* to see if you are on the "Blesseds" list.

I was a little disappointed to discover I wasn't on the list waiting to be designated a Saint. None of my friends were either. I think the reason my name isn't on the list is largely due to the fact they don't have a Patron Saint for people who write for the *Herald Republican*.

When I stop and think about it, there hasn't been a Patron Saint for a lot of things I'm interested in. Obviously there isn't one for the Chicago Cubs or their followers. My pal, Father Travis, in Chicago, says, so far there hasn't been a Saint that could hit a curve ball.

One thing I have learned is that Patron Saints don't always come when they are called. Several times I've asked for help from the Patron Saint for five card stud. I guess someone else at the table was praying harder than I was.

Then there were the times Monkey Murphy and Donald Hill used to beat up on me at recess back at Saint Paul. Back then I could have used a little help from the Patron Saint of fisticuffs. But she never showed up. I say "she" because I think the Patron Saint of fisticuffs at Saint Paul was a girl by the name of Precious Funtree. Precious could whip every kid in the school ... including Monkey Murphy and Donald Hill.

As far as school goes, I vaguely remember there was a Patron Saint for kids taking tests. Trouble is, I always forgot her name when it came around to test time.

The Curmudgeon Rides Again

"I think I shall never see anything annoying as a flea ..."
Garfield Place
Nature Is A Bitch

You know those paper placemats you see in restaurants these days? The way I see it, the ones with puzzles for the kids are okay. But what about the ones with advertising on them?

As you may well imagine, I have a few problems with paper placemats that have advertising on them. First of all, I don't understand why we even have paper placemats. Surely it can't be to hide the fact that we aren't tidy eaters. When we're through eating at restaurants that have paper placemats, the person responsible for cleaning up, either wads up the placemats or shakes the crumbs on the floor.

Carrying this used placemat scenario to its inevitable conclusion, the used placemat either ends up in the trash and gets burned, or it is shipped off to a dump somewhere. If the former is true, the burning placemat is contributing to smoke pollution. If the latter is the case, it is doubtless contributing to the growing problem of places to put bigger and bigger trash dumps.

Let's look at this paper placemat issue from a tree's point of view. If you were a big tree, would you want your little seedlings to be cut down and made into paper placemats with advertising on them?

I'm real suspicious of eateries that use placemats with advertising on them. You should be too. What's under that placemat? What are they trying to hide on the table surface? How do you know if that placemat is made out of food approved paper? What if the ink is toxic? We have all heard about the red dye problem. Do they have the same problem with red ink? Has the paper and the ink been approved by the FDA? What if the paper is made from a particular tree that has some kind of deadly tree disease? What if I walk out of that restaurant and suddenly my limbs start falling off?

Another thing that makes me suspicious about paper placemats is the kinds of firms that advertise on paper placemats. I ate at a restaurant the other day that had a paper placemat on which a funeral home was advertising. Were they trying to tell me something? Was this some kind of *Twilight Zone* thing? Out at the First Church of Big Miracles we are told to embrace the concept of predestination. Did this mean my next stop after I left the restaurant was the funeral home? If that's the case, I don't think a paper placemat is the proper way to inform me I'm on my way to the big restaurant in the sky for my last supper.

Another thing. I question why some of the firms I see advertising on paper placemats figure a paper placemat is the proper (and effective) way to spend their advertising dollar. One of the firms I'm talking about is a law firm who specializes in divorces. It said so right there on the placemat: WE SPECIALIZE IN DIVORCES.

Who wants to think about a divorce while they are eating a tuna fish sandwich? I don't want some paper placemat putting any ideas in my wife's head.

The ad the hospital decided to put on the paper placemat doesn't make a whole lot of sense either. If a person feels bad enough to go to a hospital, they probably aren't going to be sitting in a restaurant reading paper placemats. If I'm eating in a restaurant, the last thing I want to think about is going to the hospital.

I saw a paper placemat the other day that featured an advertisement by a dentist. Now there's something I really want to think about while I'm waiting for them to serve my smashed potatoes. Incidentally, this dentist mentions in his ad that he is an I. U.

The Curmudgeon Rides Again

grad. You have to hand it to this guy. He's warning you right up front that if you happened to be from Purdue or Michigan or Ohio State, he may see this as an opportunity to get even with you for some of the Saturday afternoon humiliations you have heaped on him in the past.

My favorite though is the advertisement Dr. Bob, the optometrist, put on the paper placemat. In the ad, his office telephone number was in real small print. If your eyes were bad enough you couldn't read the print; you were bound to reach the conclusion you needed his services. If you could read it, the number was small enough to make you strain your eyes and prove, once again, you needed to visit Dr. Bob.

Now that's advertising.

" ... Where did we get the idea that sound is more manageable than silence?"
Margaret Halsey
With Malice Toward None
1938

Ask someone to list the three things they absolutely dread and you are likely to hear that one of their fears is getting up in front of a group of people and giving a speech.

For years, having to stand up and speak in public was one of my worst nightmares. Many is the time I picked a seat in class behind the biggest kid in the room in the hope the teacher wouldn't see me and therefore wouldn't call on me to recite.

In college, and later, in the military, I began to learn some truths about public speaking. The most important being that if I could learn to do it, I was one step ahead of all those other folks who felt uncomfortable, intimidated, and nervous when confronted with the prospect of getting up and speaking in front of a group.

Secondly, and this, truth be known, was probably my real motivation, I had discovered something I wanted to talk about and share with others. I wanted to talk about writing. When I was talking about writing, I was okay. I wanted to share my experience with others who were interested in the craft.

Before long I evolved from someone who was terrified at the thought of getting up in front of an audience to someone who was accepting speaking engagements, doing writing seminars, teaching, giving keynote addresses ... and, in general, acting like I knew what I was doing.

So, I start this little epistle by admitting I am not an authority on giving speeches. But I have learned a few things that may help you overcome your dread of standing in front of a group and speaking.

1. If you are giving an after dinner speech, don't talk too long. Caution: Even if you are an authority on foot fungus, don't talk about something so gross that it might otherwise ruin a delightful evening for someone who came for the rubber chicken dinner and not to hear you speak.

2. Keep in mind most people have to go to the restroom following dinner. Long speeches tend to make people uncomfortable. Look for signs of people squirming in their chairs. Caution: You will feel bad if suddenly you realize half of your audience has departed to take care of nature.

3. Do not worry about how you look. Most of the folks in your audience will feel like you are looking at them during your speech and they will be concerned about how you think they look. Caution: Refrain from continually star-

ing at the prettiest woman in the audience. Her husband may not like it.

4. If you are called upon to speak at an awards banquet, make certain you are scheduled to speak before they start passing out the awards. After the various members of the audience have received their plaques and trophies they want to go home and call their mother, girlfriend, whatever, to tell them about the award they received. Listening to you speak is the last thing on their mind.

5. If you are the speaker and this is a dinner speaking engagement you will probably be sitting at the head table. This means that everyone will be watching you eat. Use your fork. Do not poke food in your mouth with your forefinger. Practice eating off of a plate before the occasion in question.

6. Try to sit next to the prettiest member of the female gender at the head table. People will be looking at her instead of you. If you sit next to the homeliest person at the head table people will take note of the fact you wipe your nose on your sleeve.

7. Prepare a few notes for the person who is going to introduce you. At many dining/speaking engagements the person that introduces you has never met you, doesn't know you, may not like you, and probably wonders why you were selected to speak to this particular group in the first place.

8. If you become involved in a question and answer period following your presentation, always repeat the question for the benefit of the other folks in the room. This takes time and it makes it appear you are thinking about how to frame your answer. If you do this it will not be so apparent that you have no idea how to respond. Actually, it

My Wife Drives A Momserati

makes no difference whether your response has anything to do with the question at hand. It will probably give you an opportunity to use a couple of the clever anecdotes you forgot to use during your speech. This speech tactic is called the "politician's response." Most speakers learned to give totally irrelevant answers by watching politicians debate.

9. Every now and then, try to insert a modest measure of humor in your speech. This accomplishes two things. If and when people in the audience laugh, you will know they are still awake. I forget what else it accomplishes.

10. If they applaud when you have finished your speech, get out of town before they figure out you weren't worth the time or the money.

"By sudden and adroit movement I placed my left eye in front of Harley Klink's fist. That's when he won the argument."
John Howsey
How To Get Along
1927

Moonbeam and I got into one of our "discussions" the other day. This particular debate centered around if you can tell whether a person is "*honest*" by what they wear.

"Give me your definition of '*honesty*,'" my long time bride challenged.

"Well," I said, " ... an honest person is someone who wears clean underwear even though they aren't going to the doctor. They are honest people because even though they know no one will have the opportunity to see that they are wearing clean underwear, they still wear it. That's real honesty."

"Wait a minute," Moonbeam gasped, "... are you saying your only test for 'honesty' in an individual is whether or not the person is wearing clean underwear?"

"Not the only test," I admitted, "... but it's as good as some of the other tests I've seen for honesty."

"And what might they be?" Moonbeam wanted to know.

"Well first we both have to agree on what an honest person really is," I insisted. "Do you agree an honest person is virtuous, moral, righteous, honorable, noble, wholesome, chaste, angelic and wears clean underwear?"

"Where did you come up with this clean underwear mania?" Moonbeam wanted to know. You can always tell when Moonbeam is moving in for the *coup de grace* in one of our discussions; she starts sprinkling our debate with psychological terms like *mania*. "I have to ask," she continued, "... are you laboring under the illusion that you have developed other sure-fire criteria for determining a person's honesty?"

At that point, and considering her stance, I was a bit reluctant to admit I had developed other barometers for determining a person's basic rectitude or mendacity. Despite my reluctance to do so I blurted out, "I think you can also tell whether a person is honest if they carry a handkerchief and avoid using their sleeve to wipe their nose."

Moonbeam was aghast. "Underwear and handkerchiefs?" she repeated, "I don't believe it."

"People can lie about a lot of things," I said, "... but only a totally honest individual will admit they did or did not change underwear or grab a clean handkerchief before they went out in the world to conquer a new day."

Moonbeam was still pondering what I had said when I

informed her I considered socks to be among the sartorial items that could be added to the "honest clothing" list.

"Why socks?" she wanted to know.

"Well, if you think about it," I said, " ... clothes cover up the underwear, the pocket hides the handkerchief, and shoes hide the socks. No one knows if the person is wearing clean underwear, uses a clean handkerchief, or is wearing dirty socks because they are all covered up by something."

"You are mentally disturbed," Moonbeam assessed. "I've never heard such jibberish."

"Want to know what other tests I apply to determine whether or not a person is honest?"

"Go ahead," she said, " ... this ought to be interesting."

"Example: I think men are not being honest when they wear long sleeve shirts to cover up a tattoo of a girl's name."

"That depends," Moonbeam groused. "If it says 'I love my wife, so and so,' he should be proud to display it."

"You're losing sight as to what this discussion is all about," I remind her. "It's about honesty and people wearing garments that either reveal their honesty or lack of it."

"Give me an example of the latter," Moonbeam insists.

"Okay," I say, " ... what about men wearing wigs. Is that honest?"

"Of course not," my bride sniffed.

"Then why should women be able to color their hair, pad their bra, and wear makeup? Is that being honest?"

"We have to do that because men have such superficial values. Men think it is more important for a woman to be attractive than bright."

"That's not how I feel," I protested. "I like Sharon Stone for her brains, not her looks."

I don't think Moonbeam bought that one either.

The Curmudgeon Rides Again

> "The very fact that we make such a to-do over golden wedding anniversaries indicates our amazement at human endurance. It is actually a recognition of stamina."
> Ilka Chase

Free Admission
1948

Every year, about this time, my bride breaks out in the shivering fits and starts talking about "our plans for the summer." Trust me, the Pentagon's plan for the invasion of Panama was less detailed than Moonbeam's approach to the good old summertime.

This year's plan includes everything from putting out a garden, to cleaning out the garage, to when and where we go on vacation.

What is this thing women have with gardens? Plow, disc, fertilize, cultivate, weed, water, and lots of sweat equals a rutabaga.

When's the last time you craved a rutabaga?

The way I see it, the ideal garden would be one where you dug a hole in the ground, dumped in a fistful of seeds, and up popped a salad with bacon bits and croutons. I wouldn't mind all the work a garden entails if you could grow stuff like lobster tails and chocolate-covered pecan clusters.

We had a garden last year. The raccoons got all the sweet corn and the rabbits got all the lettuce. Not only that, we blew twenty bucks on gasoline driving around every evening trying to palm off excess tomatoes on friends. We had the six most prolific tomato plants in all America. Six tomato plants turned our family kitchen into a tomato-canning factory.

The garden requires lots of discussion before we plant it. We don't have the right place to put a garden. West of the house is in the woods. Back of the house is a steep drop off into alligator country (I'm surprised Moonbeam still believes that one). East of the house is the septic tank. The only place that's left is the front yard. It all boils down to whether we want to plow it or mow it.

This year I voted for the little patch of ground behind the garage. If it's back there I don't have to look at it. I'm not constantly reminded that it needs to be weeded and watered.

The painting the garage project is a whole different issue. Moonbeam says we have to clean it out before we paint it. I'm not looking forward to either one of these chores. I voted we burn it ... but Moonbeam informs me her vote carries more weight than mine.

A garage is a place where some people put cars. We put "things" in our garage. Lots of things. We're missing a car somewhere. I told Moonbeam I'll bet it's hiding in there with all those "things."

The only reason we need a place for our "things" is because we never throw anything away. If I'm looking for something and Moonbeam tells me it's in the garage, it's easier to drive into town and buy a new one than lose a whole weekend looking for it.

That's how we got our last car. I had to go buy a new one because I couldn't find the old one.

When the tax assessor saw our garage he wanted to know if we were going to open an antique mall. Moonbeam said, "Yes." She said she intends to sell me.

There's some suspicion that the neighbor's teenage son

The Curmudgeon Rides Again

has been lost in our garage for the last couple of years. I told his parents not to worry. He'll eventually find his way out if he has any tenacity.

Assuming we get our chores done on schedule, Moonbeam and I then plan to take a vacation. I prefer a dual-purpose vacation. I define "dual purpose" where I can do a little research on my next book and relax. Moonbeam also prefers a dual-purpose vacation. For Moonbeam that's any place where you can shop both day and night.

We always vote on where we go. I'm voting for the rockbound coast of Maine or Newfoundland. Moonbeam is thinking Florida. I think we're going to Florida.

Actually, I'm happy that Moonbeam plans these things out. I mean, if she didn't, I'd probably end up lying on the pontoon boat all summer, soaking up the sun, enjoying a good book, fixing dinner on the bar-b-que, and enjoying myself.

But, back to reality, and the garage, and the ...

A Tatterdemalion Testimony To Technology

Henry Ford once said he didn't care whether a man came from Harvard or Sing Sing. "We hire a man, not his history."

Good old Henry may have gotten away with that hiring philosophy back when he was setting up his first assembly line, but I hardly think he would be so cavalier about education in this day and age of technology. As Alvin Toffler pointed out, "Technology feeds on itself. Technology makes more technology possible."

I can attest to that fact because each day that goes by that I haven't quite caught up with the old technology, I fall further behind on evolving technology. That's the way the world works these days.

You will better understand when I tell you the following is a true story ... related just the way it happened.

To begin with, nowhere in all the land is there anyone (specifically me) less qualified to write what my editors and publisher like to call "technothrillers." I have difficulty changing lightbulbs. It is a monumental achievement for me to successfully change the

The Curmudgeon Rides Again

ribbon on my printer or put the key in the ignition right side up.

As a high school student I had trouble with commercial arithmetic and every level of mathematics that followed. I was able to pass high school physics and chemistry only because the girl sitting next to me wrote really large. Bless her unsuspecting soul. Or, perhaps she knew of my desperate straits and felt sorry for me. Whichever, it didn't take me long to figure out that in order to move on (academically) I had to sit next to the aforementioned young lady in science and math classes.

Later, in college, I worked hard to achieve a Bachelor of Arts degree instead of a Bachelor of Science degree. Proving once again, discretion is indeed the better part of valor. If I had been forced to face a college curriculum that included a variety of college math and science courses, I would still be in college trying to figure out a way to beat the system.

Why am I telling you all of this? Because, as some of you already know, my last 12 novels, beginning with *Red Tide* in 1992 through the most recent, *The Search for Sebastian Rainer* (to be released late in 2002) have all had a strong technological orientation. Telling you how this all came about is not only somewhat amusing, it also gives you some insight as to how the publishing industry works.

I sold my first novel, a sinister fiction effort, in 1984. Between 1984 and 1991 I was able to sell nine more novels, all written along the Stephen King line. (Hey, if you're going to follow in someone's footsteps, why not the man who has sold more copies of more books than any other novelist in history.) Then, one day, while dreaming up plots ominous and ill-omened, I received the phone call that changed everything.

My then editor at Dorchester Publishing, John Littell, called and informed me that he wanted me to develop a story line based on something he had "thought up" while riding the train into the city that morning (New York).

A Tatterdamalion Testimony To Technology

"This plane takes off from a secret air base about eight o'clock on a Monday morning," John said, " ... then it lands on Friday afternoon and in the meantime a whole bunch of really bad stuff has happened to it. What do you think?" he concluded.

"That's it?" I questioned.

"Great idea, huh? Think you can do anything with it?"

"Are you forgetting," I stalled, "I'm one of your sinister fiction writers."

"I'm moving you into a whole new field," John said, " ... it's called 'technothrillers'."

"Never heard of it," I admitted.

"That's because I just thought up the name," John said.

To make what is now a fun story to reflect back on, John told me to think about it, and get back to him with a story line. It took two weeks but I did. *Red Tide* was born, and in the process gave birth to a whole series of *Red* books with my publisher (seven at last count).

So there you have it, a writer who can barely spell the word "technology" is now writing about some of the military's most sophisticated equipment. Even though my writing library is skewed heavily to books geared toward the technological reader these days, the telling of a good story steeped in things technical is still accomplished primarily with old story telling skills evolving out of ideas hastily jotted on paper.

Here then is my tatterdemalion testimony to technology.

The Curmudgeon Rides Again

"Writing is easy: all you have to do is sit staring at the blank sheet of paper until drops of blood form on your forehead."
—Ring Lardner

The other day someone asked what I thought it took to become a writer. To be specific, their question was, "What is the one essential skill a person must have to make a go of it in writing?"

A thought provoking question.

I gave the matter considerable lucubration before I even attempted to answer her.

"On balance," I said, " ... I am convinced the most important thing you have to know how to do in order to be a writer is stare." By that I mean, "staring" as one would do if they were looking intently at a blank wall.

A good writer finds blank walls interesting. If you are the kind who just gapes or gawks or rubber necks at a blank wall, people will immediately know that you are not a writer and that you are only a pretend-to-be-writer. Pretend-to-be-writers wear an expression on their face which is designed to make observers think they are thinking of something.

Real writers don't wear discernible expressions. Real writers don't even know why they are staring. In most cases they aren't even aware that they are staring.

I have been writing professionally for 18 years now and it has taken me a long time to learn to stare properly. For a while I tried doing it with my eyes closed. This is called "closed eye staring." I found this practice to be somewhat unsatisfactory be-

A Tatterdamalion Testimony To Technology

cause I frequently fell asleep. Despite the obviousness of the blank wall, people tend to know when you are not really staring and are only pretending to stare. That's because they can hear you snoring.

When "closed eye staring" proved unsatisfactory, I embraced the French school of "alternate eye staring." In "alternate eye staring" the individual attempts to stare with one eye while permitting the other eye to do what it wants to do. Unfortunately, this method proved to be unsatisfactory as well.

It wasn't until I mastered the patented two-eye stare known in the writer's stare manual as the "blank look" that I felt I was really on my way to mastering this first important step toward becoming a writer. Even today, conquering both Staring 101 and Staring 102 presents many newcomers to the field of writing with a daunting challenge.

The novice starer will often ask, how do I know I have mastered the staring aspect of my writing career? How do I know I am ready to move on to the second phase of my writing career? Answer: Frankly it is difficult to tell. However, there are two behaviors on the part of those who are actually observing your staring technique that will often give you a clue as to how proficient you have become in your endeavors.

1. If people stop and look at the wall to see what you are staring at, you deserve a D for your efforts.
2. If they stop to see if you have conveyed any of the images they think you

are staring at to words on paper, you have successfully passed the staring requirements for a writer. Usually a simple word such as "cat" scrawled on your sheet of paper will be enough to convince the avid writer observer that you are indeed one of the writing species.

In order to prove you are a time-tested, money-making, real professional writer, you will have to scrawl something a bit more complicated on your paper. Something like "big cat" will usually be sufficient.

In mastering staring exercises to become a writer, one can usually expedite the learning curve by using the patented "Stare Master," a device that greatly enhances staring exercises.

The "Stare Master" projects images on the wall. Staring at these images will (the "Stare Master" claims) help you stimulate your imagination and give you ideas. This in turn, according to the Stare Master, will help you become the kind of writer doing the kind of writing you think you will be interested in writing when you have the staring aspect of writing down pat.

A less obvious benefit of learning to stare properly is that it is an exercise that enables you to get used to your writing glasses. Writers who wear the coolest glasses are the writers who wear half-glasses. By looking first through the half-lens and then over the half-lens you learn to view things, matters, issues, from two different perspectives. Being able to view matters from two different perspectives, of course, is not necessary if you intend to write about politics or religion.

More important, however, is the fact you exercise your eyes by moving them up and down while you are practicing staring.

In addition there are several things you should not do while you are practicing staring. Never whistle, sing songs, or doodle on a piece of paper while staring. People will think you are not completely engrossed in your staring (hence not a professional) or they will think you are doing spirit writing.

Bottom line: Look, act, dress like a writer, but folks will not believe you are one until you prove you can stare.

A Tatterdamalion Testimony To Technology

> "I love being a writer. What I can't stand is the paper work."
> —Peter de Vries

After informing the woman that learning to stare properly was the most essential requirement for becoming a writer, she promptly asked me what came after staring. The answer, of course, as to the second most important thing in becoming a writer is to learn to master "the tools of writing."

But first, now that you know how proficient you must be at staring to become a writer, let's talk about what kind of results you can expect from successful staring. If, for example, in the initial stages of your staring career, you tend to see images on the wall, you should probably give some thought to becoming a psychic rather than a writer. If you persist in seeing images and still wish to become a writer, perhaps you should consider becoming a psychic writer. If you see full-blown stories on the wall when you are staring ... it is probably because someone covered the wall with newspapers.

In prior days, writers would walk by my desk, see me staring at the wall and whisper things like, "He's learning to be a writer but he doesn't quite have his staring down yet." When I heard remarks such as these, I knew I wasn't ready for the second stage of my writing career. But, after years of hard practice, I finally did learn to stare convincingly.

At that point I was ready to move onto the second phase of my writing career development: learning to use the tools of

The Curmudgeon Rides Again

writing. The technical term for the most important tool in the writer's arsenal is "pencil." Early in my career I tried a number of different "pencils" before I found one that fit my personality. Then, one day I found a "yellow pencil." Since then I have learned that the "yellow pencil" is an extremely versatile writing tool and most writing professionals view it as a good training model. It can be operated dull or sharp, wet or dry, and the deluxe model has an eraser on it. If you are a new writer, an eraser will come in handy.

A piece of advice. Do not be overwhelmed by the many features of a good "yellow pencil." Like all complicated tools, the novice should learn to operate and master one feature at a time. People can tell a great deal about a writer by their pencil. As my writing teacher often said, "Pencils are good."

After the pencil comes "paper." "Paper," like the aforementioned "pencil," comes in a number of shapes, sizes, and textures. You will soon discover "paper" to be a handy item when embracing the profession of writing. In addition to the features mentioned previously, paper comes in sheets or rolls. You can make your own paper if you are a friend of trees. However, homemade paper is often lumpy. The paper with horizontal lines on it is my favorite although most any type of paper will do, except, of course, toilet paper.

It has been my experience that both facial tissue and toilet tissue are too thin and will tear rather easily when you try to write on it. However, if you do most of your writing in the bathroom that kind of paper is always handy.

Paper sacks from the grocery store are also very good for writing because you can erase what you have written several times before the paper shreds. This, of course, will depend on whether or not you have selected a "yellow pencil" with an "eraser" as one of your writing tools.

For the writer who is not all that familiar with words, I suggest a spelling book (not a dictionary). Dictionaries are for

A Tatterdamalion Testimony To Technology

looking up the meaning of words and when you are trying to accumulate lots of words, it is not necessary to know what they mean.

A spelling book will accomplish two things. One, it will present you with lots of words. Two, it will tell you how to spell them. For writers, just knowing there is a word that stands for something is not sufficient; you must know how to spell the word. In the event you do not feel like spending fifteen or twenty dollars on a spelling book, and providing you know people with children, you can always borrow their spelling book. Most children will be happy to lend you their spelling book if you promise not to return it.

Having accomplished all of the above, you are now ready to try writing a few words or perhaps even a sentence. Over the years I have become somewhat spoiled by modern writing conveniences such as a flat writing surface and sufficient lighting ... and we will talk about them in an upcoming piece of "learning how to become a writer."

"My editor told me he thought my manuscript was both good and original. The problem was the parts that were good were not original and the parts that were original were not good."
—Samuel Johnson

Recently we have been discussing writers and the tools of technology one must master if one expects to become a writer.

The Curmudgeon Rides Again

We began by discussing the necessity of developing the ability to stare convincingly at a blank wall to make people think you are conjuring up convoluted plots. We even went so far as to say you must learn to stare convincingly or people will not believe you are developing a plot.

Next we discussed the importance of understanding state-of-the-art technical equipment like pencils, papers, and erasers. You can always tell a real writer. Real writers display bumper stickers that say, "I love pencils."

Our in-depth review of technical equipment was followed by pointing out that writers need to learn lots of "words." It is important to note that we also stressed that it was not necessary to know the meaning of those words, because, as we learned in our composition classes in both high school and college, it is not how you use the word, it matters only that you use a certain number of them. That is why most pages in most books have a lot of words on them.

Before we go into our third and final phase of "getting ready to become a writer," I would like to mention two other things that I believe will be helpful to the novice in this endeavor.

Let's start with the writing surface, the place where you will learn to put some of the words you have learned on paper.

Ideally, you will find a flat place to write. Tables, desks, butcher blocks, floors, ceilings, walls, if properly maintained will serve this purpose.

Another helpful hint I feel compelled to offer new writers has to do with proper illumination. Early on in my career, I wrote out on the garage apron under the security light. This proved to be unsatisfactory. Bugs are drawn to security lights. You may experiment if you wish, but writing inside will more than likely prove to be most satisfactory.

If you have survived, managed to hurdle, taken in stride and have not as yet been over-whelmed by the aforementioned

A Tatterdamalion Testimony To Technology

technological hurdles to becoming a writer ... and you are still entertaining thoughts of devoting your life to that profession, listening to what others have to say about the subject of being a writer will certainly be of help.

F. Scott Fitzgerald said, " ... Writing is like swimming under water and being obliged to hold your breath while doing so." I believe the analogy is obvious.

John Kenneth Galbraith wrote, "Originality is something that is easily exaggerated, especially by authors who are contemplating and assessing their own work."

Harcord Marx said the same thing about originality.

I am told that one writer of considerable experience had this bit of advice for a new writer. "Don't sit down to write if you haven't had some experience standing up to life." Red Skelton said, "Don't sit down to write if you haven't got a chair."

Gene Fowler and Rod Serling are both reported to have said, "Writing is easy. All you have to do is stare at a piece of blank paper until you break out in a cold sweat and then call your editor to see if he has an idea for you to develop."

Hemingway once said, "If you want to be a writer have some other skill you can use to make enough money so that you can eat regularly while you are learning to write." Or, work in a restaurant where your meals are free.

The originator of this bit of wisdom is unknown. 'Writers seldom write about the things they think. Most of them write about the things they think other folks think they think."

The Curmudgeon Rides Again

A gem from one of my early writing instructors: "Nature, when she invented, designed, manufactured and patented writers, had some scraps left over. In an effort to make judicious use of all the left over materials, she created critics."

And for that small handful of you who may have become enchanted with this wonderful art form and are reluctant to start ...

Nature fits all her children with something to do ...

He who would write and can't write, can surely review. They can set up small booths as critic and sell us their Petty conceits and pettier jealousies.

... Now, all you have to do to get started is stare at the wall while fondling your pencil, stroking your paper, and recalling a few words.

Ain't writing fun?

"One way I save energy is by asking my servants not to turn on the self-cleaning ovens during peak power demand periods."
attributed to Betty Bloomingdale

To the precious few of you who stumble across this curmudgeonly column every now and then, it will come as no surprise when I tell you that, on occasion, I tend to have an opinion or two on some of the world's weightier issues.

Well, rules and regulation fans, today I have an opinion about "licenses" and "licensing agencies."

If you drive a car, you have to have a driver's license.

If you fly a plane, you need a pilot's license.

If you practice medicine, you have to have a license.

In fact, it takes a license to cut hair, go fishing, hunt, teach, carry a gun, etc. How many more examples do you need?

Although the answer is fairly obvious, we license people do all of the above (and a whole lot more) only after the individual in question has demonstrated acceptable levels of proficiency performing the task at hand. (Let's not get picky out there in reader land ... I've got a point to make.)

So ... why don't we license people to use telephones? Quick, can you think of any modern day convenience that is more abused?

I think people ought to have to pass some sort of "intelligence use" test before the store is permitted to sell them a telephone. The way things are now, telephones have become instruments of social decay.

Say "Amen," brother!

Let's face it, if you have a mouth, you can use a phone ... and those are usually the ones that get them first.

The minute you get a telephone, the quality of life begins to deteriorate. What happens? First you get phone calls during the dinner hour. These calls are obviously from someone who isn't eating. More often than not they are from someone who is trying to sell you light bulbs, bananas, or a subscription to *Better Dining*. Is it necessary to point out that you'll dine a whole lot better if you simply take the phone off the hook?

The folks who set up telemarketing campaigns design them so that the majority of their calls are made during dinner hour.

The Curmudgeon Rides Again

Their thinking is the recipient of the call will buy just about anything just so they can get off the phone and eat their dinner before the food spoils.

But it's not just the "incoming calls" that are annoying. "Outgoing calls" can be pretty much the same. After dinner, our teenage daughter disappears into her own little time-warped corner of the world and spends the rest of the evening on the telephone. Who in the name of Alexander Graham Bell is she talking to? If I called everyone I've ever met and read them all seven volumes of Will Durant's *The History of Civilization* I could not possibly spend that much time on the telephone.

Our daughter had her picture taken for her high school yearbook without a telephone plastered to the side of her head and no one in the family recognized her.

There was an article in the paper the other day about a woman who wanted to be buried with her telephone. Can you imagine? Does she know something the average phone user doesn't know? What if she can actually call people?

Heaven forbid! I'll bet even hell would forbid!

Think about getting a call from a lady in a casket in the middle of the night. That'll put a fizz back in your stale pop.

Actually, this particular situation poses some unique problems. For example, how does the phone company collect on her phone bill? If she doesn't pay her bill on time can a dead person get a bad credit rating? Is this what we would call a "dead beat?"

Teenagers aren't the only ones who should have to be licensed before they are allowed to use a telephone. Bosses should also be licensed. Actually, bosses should be required to get two licenses. First, they should have to demonstrate that they can pass the yelling, screaming, and employee degrading test. Otherwise how do we know they are qualified to be a boss? Then they should be required to get a special boss's telephone license before they are permitted to call you at home on a Friday night to ask

A Tatterdamalion Testimony To Technology

you to work on a Saturday.

I made a list of people who, before they are permitted to use a telephone with any degree of frequency, should have to pass a "telephone use test." We can start with teenagers, bosses, people driving cars, telemarketing types, and people who eat in restaurants. When I see someone using a cell phone in a restaurant, I'm tempted to walk over to their table and say, "Yes, everyone sees you. We all know you are here. We all recognize how important you must be. Plus, we all know there isn't anyone on the other end of the line, so why don't you just put your phone away and eat your soup?"

Who should be able to operate a telephone without having to obtain a license first? Well, let's start a list. How about doctors (they really need phones, because most people can't read their writing)? Then comes the police, the fire department, the hospital ... and maybe the President of the United States. But the ones at the top of the list should be writers. After all, we have to call our agents.

> ## "Television, like technology, feeds on itself. That's why it so often has indigestion."
> ### attributed to Walter Cronkite

Look around. I'd be willing to bet that if you can see ten or more people from where you are standing, you see ten people who have accepted modern technology more gracefully than I have.

The Curmudgeon Rides Again

When someone starts using state-of-the-art buzzwords to describe the features on some new electronic gizmo, I tend to get a little hyper. Does using a palm pilot mean I can fly my hand? Or just exactly what is an "interactive multimedia device?" Does it mean there is some new gadget on the market that will enable me to read the newspaper, listen to the radio, watch television, and get sick to my stomach all at the same time? That's the way I normally "interact" with all the depressing stuff that's printed, programmed, promulgated and presented.

In my opinion, our toys, tools, and trifles are getting much, much too complicated. Whatsmore, this whole subject of complex technology just became even more confusing with the announcement that a whole new cadre of telephone services are being made available to us. Now, for example, we can rent or purchase what the techno-freaks call "smart telephones."

Smart telephones? I was happy with the dumb ones.

My friend Techno Tom tells me they call them "smart" because these new plastic marvels are actually capable of making choices for us.

Now if there is one thing I absolutely do not need, it is something else hanging around the house that's going to make choices for me. With one wife, five children, a mother-in-law, and Uncle Know-It-All, making life decisions for me already, I don't need a "smart telephone." I might actually be capable of making better decisions if I were given the chance to practice by making a few.

I saw a phone with a lot of buttons the other day. Lots of buttons and blinking lights means it's high-tech. On one of the phones you can give the friendly folks down at the phone company the numbers of 10 people whose call you want to be put through immediately. In other words, they get the VIP treatment. At the same time, you can give them the phone numbers of 10 people you don't want to hear from. This is called "call block-

A Tatterdamalion Testimony To Technology

ing."

First of all, I don't know 10 VIP's ... so I don't need that service. Secondly, I can think of at least 241 people I would like to have blocked. Ten just isn't enough. I tried to sort through the list to see if I could come up with the ten top names of callers I don't want to hear from. Two hundred and forty-one people tied for first.

Long before the telephone company developed their high-tech "call blocking" service, I had one of my own. I would pick up the receiver and say hello in Chinese. By the time the caller stumbled around and mumbled his or her way through a few apologies for dialing the wrong number, I usually had a pretty good idea who it was and whether or not I wanted to talk to them. If I didn't, I simply kept up the stream of Chinese chatter until they hung up in frustration. If it was someone I wanted to talk to, I paused, cleared my throat, and apologized for my Chinese houseboy's poor English. It worked just fine and it didn't cost me an extra four or five dollars for the "call screening" device.

In addition to the services I've already mentioned, the new fancy twenty-four button telephone with all the blinking lights offers a call forwarding service. In theory you give the phone company the number where you expect to be. Then the call is forwarded from where the caller called you to the place where you said you would be when the call came through ... unless, of course, you are delayed or for some reason never got to the place where the call was forwarded.

If that happens, the state police are alerted and you are either assisted or arrested for giving the phone company false information. Inevitably though, you will be standing at church, drinking your coffee after services, when someone in the congregation walks up to you and says, "I see the police stopped you ... speeding again, huh?"

"No," you say, " ... they stopped me because I had a very

important phone call."

"Yeah, sure," the person snickers and walks away.

According to the brochure the phone company gave me, you can obtain a phone capable of and then sign up for the automatic caller I.D., automatic redial, automatic call return, automatic call blocking, automatic VIP alert, automatic call-forwarding, automatic call screening, automatic announcing services, and automatic halitosis detection. There is even a way to pick up your e-mail and other messages left on your computer. The whole bevy of services can add as much as an additional fifty to seventy-five dollars to your monthly telephone bill.

Or ... for a whole lot less, I can teach you how to sound like a Chinese houseboy with very poor English.

> "The seat of the soul and the control of voluntary movement ... in fact, of all nervous functions in general ... are to be sought in the heart. The brain is an organ of minor importance."
> Aristotle
> *De motu animalium*
> 4th century B.C.

I'll let you in on a secret. Writers hate (with a passion) to be interrupted when they are writing. And the most frequent of maddening interruptions are spawned by that instrument of the

A Tatterdamalion Testimony To Technology

devil: The telephone.

Etch this in stone. This is a big deal with writers: Most writers feel that any intrusion on their writing time is a very big and very unpopular occurrence.

With most of us who get paid by the word or book, it doesn't matter whether it's Federal Express, an unexpected visit from an old acquaintance or a phone call. It ain't welcome. Writers view interlopers as unwelcome invasions, monumental interferences, and intolerable disruptions.

Let's face it, when you're blowing up the Kremlin, or fending off the fiendish attack of some terrorist group, the last thing you want to do is put the whole episode on hold while you commiserate with Uncle Harold about his bunions or his latest girlfriend.

Why am I bringing this up?

Because the other day I was right in the middle of an important ship wreck scene for my latest novel when the telephone rang.

"Are you the owner of the house at _____?" a nasal voice intoned.

Immediately recognizing this as another one of the true scourges of the millennium, a & % * telemarketing call, I informed the caller that I wasn't the owner and gave them the name and address of the bank that holds the mortgage on our humble domicile. Then I hung up.

Less than ten minutes later, and no further along with resolving my fictional crises involving pounding waves, violent winds, and sinking ships (because I had been rudely interrupted and completely lost my train of thought), the phone rings again.

"Hi, Mr. Largent," an overly friendly, somewhat syrupy voice greets me, " ... hope you're having a nice day."

"Do I know you?" I question.

"My name is *mumble mumble* with the *mumble mumble* Fruit Company and we're checking with all of our old customers (despite *mumble mumble's* overt familiarity, I am certain I have never heard of the *mumble mumble* Fruit Company), to see if they would be interested in our special on kumquats."

"The *mumble mumble* Fruit Company," I repeat, "... say, aren't you the ones I'm suing for shipping me a crate of spoiled kumquats?" All of which results in a fast disconnect and in no time at all I'm back at the old computer trying to cope with a storm tossed sinking vessel.

Ring. Ring. This time the caller wants to "speak with the lady of the house."

"Me too," I whine, "but she ain't here no more. She ran off with a door-to-door refrigerator salesman a couple of weeks ago. Ain't heard hide nor hair of her since."

Silence on the other end of the line.

"Say, you wouldn't be that refrigerator fella, would ya?" I question.

Disconnect and back to work. At the rate I'm going, the ship will have sunk, everyone will have died, and the storm will have passed ... which isn't much of an adventure yarn.

A half hour later I'm downstairs trying to conjure up one of my culinary favorites, a peanut butter sandwich with onions, when the phone rings again.

This one wants to speak to "the lady of the house," too. (Don't telemarketers know that bra burners don't want members of their gender referred to as *ladies*?)

"Well," I drawl, "... she's out back making opossum sausage. We got us some real fine road kill this morning and she's trying to get it cooked before it spoils ..."

Silence. Finally I hear a click. Back to what's left of the boat.

The phone rings again.

A Tatterdamalion Testimony To Technology

I snap it up (I'm a slow learner). This time it's one of the credit card companies offering "a very low 1.9% introductory rate on a Visa or MasterCard" because "I've been preapproved."

"How much can I get?" I shout with glee. "I'm sure glad you called. I'm in hock up to my ears. Every bank in town has turned me down and six of my credit cards are maxed out. If you can lend me a quick thirty thousand on this new card, it'll solve all my problems this month."

Click.

Moments later the phone rings again. It's my editor. "Been tryin' to get through for hours. Beats me how you get any writing done the way you're always jawin' on the phone."

> "I have a simple philosophy.
> Fill what is empty.
> Empty what is full.
> And scratch where it itches."
> Alice Roosevelt Longworth
> *How to Get Through Life*

Numbers and I just don't seem to get along. We never have. Going as far back as my prep school days, my brain and any form of mathematics are like a bad marriage.

This condition has become increasingly disturbing in the last few years because more and more numbers seem to be influencing my day to day activities. Everywhere I go, everything I do, and everything I want to do, seems to involve numbers.

Take our oldest son for example. His office is in California. I asked him to send me a number where I could get in touch with him. He sent me nine numbers. There was the private line into his office, his company phone, his cell phone, E-mail, voice mail, and fax number. In addition there were three phone lines into his home. By the time I catch up with him, I usually forget why I called him.

Why does this bother me?

Well, in addition to the fact that the reason I was trying to contact him might have been important, the simple fact is I can't remember numbers. The only way I can remember a number is to write it down and carry it with me. I carry so many numbers around in my wallet there is no room for anything else. I used to carry pictures of my wife and each of our offspring around with me.

No more. Now all I carry is phone numbers.

There was a time when I used to carry money in my wallet ... but I don't do that anymore either. Now I just try to make certain I'm running around with people that have money when I go to lunch.

There toward the end, when I was running out of space in my billfold, I had to make a choice between carrying a picture of Moonbeam and a twenty dollar bill with Jackson's picture on it. After I spent the twenty dollars, I put Moonbeam's picture back in my wallet.

As I write this I'm carrying around credit card numbers, a pin number, a Social Security number, a military specialty code number, my E-mail number, my driver's license with all kinds of numbers, the prescription for my glasses, the dates I'll be off next Christmas, the last date my agent called me, the price of a new Ferrari (that's a really big number), how many calories there are in a Snickers bar, phone numbers for all our kids, and a number indicating how much money I would be carrying in my wallet if I

A Tatterdamalion Testimony To Technology

didn't have to carry all those other numbers.

My desk is even worse. I have five of those nifty books where you keep people's business cards. Each of them has several numbers. Have you noticed? Nowadays, most business cards have people's phone numbers, fax, E-mail numbers, street address and zip code. I saw a card the other day with 57 numbers on it. There were so many numbers they forgot to put the man's name on the card.

I called the alumni office of my alma mater the other day. I needed some information. They asked me what year I graduated. I didn't have the number in my billfold, so I hung up.

I called the bank. I told them who I was and asked them a question. They wanted to know my account number. I read off all the numbers at the bottom of my check. That's when they said they only needed the last six numbers. If they only needed the last six numbers, then what's the purpose of all those other numbers in front of the last six numbers?

I wanted to see if a certain book was available so I called the library. "Do you have the Library of Congress number?" the woman asked.

"Nope," I said, "but I'm certain you can find it in the Washington, D.C. phone book." I should have told her that at my age I am lucky I can even remember the title of the book.

Have you tried to buy tires recently? I did. The first thing the tire guy asked me was what kind of tire I wanted. I told him I preferred round ones but that didn't satisfy him. He wanted to know the size. How should I know which number on the side of the tire is the size? Did you ever look at your tires? There are lots of numbers on a tire. If the number is upside down it's hard to read.

Hey, if there is nothing we can do about this numbers thing, I guess I'll just have to accept it. The way it's going though, it

The Curmudgeon Rides Again

looks like we'll soon be dumping good, old-fashioned words and going to numbers as our standard way of communicating. If that happens, I think it's going to take some of the zip out of things.

Instead of saying, "I love you," you'll say, "Fourteen, thirty-one, twelve, nine, seven, forty-one, and two."

Doesn't have the same punch, does it?

Machismo Is Not An Italian Cheese

Margaret Mead once said, "A man's role in society is uncertain, undefined, and, in the view of many, totally unnecessary."

I disagree. Men just aren't mysteriously arcane like women. What you see in a man is what you get. For example, men belch and emit other gastro-intestinal noises because relief is to be desired more than refined and continued suffering. Women handle that situation more discreetly.

Men don't shave because whiskers simply don't bother them half as much as they do the women who have to look at them. Men, unlike women, have a lot of trouble with the color pink. Pink, to most men, is a sissy color.

More to the point, if the truth be known, most men don't know how to act or what to say most of the time. As one very respected member of the opposite gender once put it, "Most of the time, men are just plain asleep at the switch."

Enough of an intro? Now, at least, you know what most of the columns are about in this section: men and their behavior ... men and their often feeble responses to the fact that they must somehow find a way to get along in the world.

Perhaps this is as good a place as any to also mention that when one lady heard I was undertaking this book project, she suggested I call these mostly previously published musings "essays."

Essays? Come on. No way. To me, the word "essay"

sounds way, way too formal. To me, the word "essay" is a reminder of "composition" class and Sister Arnulfa. You remember Sister Arnulfa, don't you? She's the one I fed to the giant slugs in the basement of that old, run-down academy in my book *Pagoda*. Besides, I like the term "column." It sounds just a bit phallic. Don't you think?

So, I'm starting this little opus by readily admitting that men aren't the brightest creatures to roam the planet. Okay? I feel certain that if half of the population on earth is women, then half of the population will agree with me.

In many cases men simply don't know what to say or do. In a larger number of cases, men simply don't think. Take the time my brother-in-law, an honest, God-fearing man in his sixties, took his mother (then in her eighties) to *Hooters* for lunch. Talk about not thinking.

Still haven't proved my point? How about the time my thirty-something nephew took his parents to see the Broadway musical *Hair*? Would you like to guess how embarrassed he was when all the nude dancers began cavorting around on the stage? Would you like to guess how his parents felt?

Want more? How about the time a middle school English teacher (male) took his seventh grade class to see the movie *Pulp Fiction*? No less than six parents transferred their offspring to a nearby parochial school after that jaundiced and ill-conceived little episode.

> "I only like two kinds of r
> domestic and foreign.
> Mae West

My wife is one of those caring people. I mean this woman cares about everything: the environment, the plight of the homeless, the missions' effort of our church ... and she even cares about my teeth. How do I know my teeth are a high priority with this woman? Because she is always calling some dentist to arrange dental appointments.

Let's get down to some gut level honesty here. In my book, going to the dentist ranks right up there in popularity and elation with a visit to the Internal Revenue Service and rejection slips from publishers.

I've always attributed my lack of fondness for dentists to the fact my wife usually hooks yours truly up to some tooth inspector who learned the profession from a snake oil peddler who cleaned furnaces when he wasn't cleaning teeth. The last dentist we had before moving back to Lake Gage received his diploma from The Sheboygan School of Dentistry and Roof Repair. The guy was a former Green Bay Packer tight end who extracted most of his patients' teeth with a forearm shiver.

Say what you want. Call me a sis, but I'm wary (read that "real wary") of dentists who make house calls wearing leather tool belts packing lock grip pliers and a 3/8 inch Black and Decker variable speed drill.

"I made an appointment for you to get your teeth cleaned," the woman in my life announces, " ... on Monday."

"Monday isn't a good day for me," I inform bride-person. "I'm planning to paint the Washington Monument. I'll be tied up most of the day."

"Then you'll have to call the dentist and reschedule," I'm informed.

I hate it when she gives me all that adult-type responsibility. Nevertheless, I do as I am told. Why? Because that's what men are supposed to do, follow orders.

"Hey," I say, calling the dentist's office. "I need to reschedule my Monday appointment. Unfortunately, the only free time I have is between two-thirty and three o'clock on Sunday morning. I don't suppose that works for you, right?"

"We could manage that," the chief scheduler assures me, " ... but why don't you just come in when your wife scheduled your appointment?" My bride thinks of everything. The people in the dentist's office have been alerted.

"I'll come if you have plenty of industrial strength pain-killer," I whimper.

"You're only scheduled to have your teeth cleaned, Mr. Largent. As a rule we don't give pain-killer when we clean your teeth."

"Here's the deal," I say (I know how to negotiate; I watch every episode of *Law and Order*.), "I want two liters of Novocain the minute I walk through your door. None of this waiting until I get in the chair stuff. You either numb me before you take me back to the operating room or I'm taking hostages."

"We'll handle it," she promised.

When Monday arrived, I was still vacillating. Would they believe me if I told them President Bush needed me in the oval office to work out the details for a big Russian grain deal? Probably not.

What if I told them our dog ate our car and I didn't have any other way of getting there?

What if I told them I had an "out of body" experience and I couldn't get back in my body in time to make my appointment?

I tried all three excuses. None of them worked.

Machismo Is Not An Italian Cheese

When my time came and there was no hope of escape, I tied a bandanna over my eyes and allowed myself to be led into the inner-sanctum of tooth decay and root canals. Someone slipped a head set over my ears, cranked up the volume, and somewhere off in the distance I heard someone say, "Open your mouth."

"This is it, Lord," I whimpered. "I'm coming to get my reward. Open the gates wide." With the strains of Beethoven's 7th Symphony ringing in my ears, I spiraled down into the dark tunnel of eternal blackness.

Then I heard someone say, "That wraps it up, Mr. Largent. You're done."

"Already?" I chirp.

"Uh huh," she nodded. " ... you fell asleep."

"That's the way it is with us macho types," I crowed.

No way was I going to admit I was worn out from staying up all night trying to figure out a way of getting out of my appointment.

Margaret Mead on Ralph Waldo Emerson's assertion that, "A man ought to compare advantageously with a river, an oak tree, and a mountain." "They just don't," she said.

Let me make a categorically inclusive statement. Men, plain old ordinary every day type men, are very uneasy answering survey questions. When we respond to survey questions we go into it knowing that eventually they will put our responses in a data pool with the replies of everyone else taking the same survey. We also realize this survey is probably sponsored by some women's magazine who will use our answers to support their contention that men are a bunch of lump lumps and thoughtless clods. But we do it anyway because, for the most part, we are a bunch of lump lumps and thoughtless clods.

All of which gets me around to asking the question, how much information do they really want on these surveys? One word answers? A complete sentence? Do they want me to be brief as possible? Or, are they looking for in-depth responses that will give them insight as well as information?

Take the survey questionnaire I was given the other day. Question number 8 said: *Sleep?*

This is one of those questions that can be answered several different ways. Do they want me to say *yes*? Or how about *usually*? Maybe what they really want to know is how I do it. Maybe I should have told them in more detail about my sleep habits such as *when I sleep, more often than not it is in the prone position with my eyes closed.*

See? It all depends on what the survey takers are looking for. Are they looking for in-depth answers or just for certain key words?

Question 9 was equally perplexing. It said: *Aspirations?* This was another one of those questions that could be answered in several different ways. Any answer I gave them depended on what stage of my life they were talking about. For example, when I was young, my aspiration was to grow up to be a watermelon. Why a watermelon? Because every time I went to a party they usually had a watermelon. In my young mind I equated having fun and parties with watermelon. So, why not grow up to be one?

It wasn't until I realized that being a watermelon wasn't the end-all of end-alls that I changed my aspiration and went for something a bit more flamboyant. I think it was somewhere around my seventh birthday that I decided I wanted to be a super hero.

But which one?

At the time, super heroes were on a short list. There was Superman, Captain Marvel, Wonder Woman, and Spy Smasher. I guess that I should admit I never harbored any secret desire to be Wonder Woman ... for a couple of obvious reasons.

There were also problems with becoming Captain Marvel (I hated lightning) and Spy Smasher. On the surface, Spy Smasher was a piece of cake. All I really needed to make me look like Spy Smasher was a leather helmet, a pair of goggles, a cool cape, and a ray gun. All sartorial items I figured I was capable of attaining or talking my mother into making. But there was one significant problem. I didn't know what a *spy* was. As my mother pointed out when informed of my dilemma, if you're going to smash something you better know what it looks like. Right?

So much for Spy Smasher.

Superman, however, turned out to be a real possibility. Why? Because they sold Superman outfits at Woolworth's. I saw 'em. For a buck ninety-eight you could get a genuine Superman top with a big "s" on the chest, Superman shorts, a Superman cape, and red plastic things you could wrap around your legs so it would look like you were wearing Superman boots.

After much pleading, cajoling, and groveling, I was able to talk my mother into a complete Superman outfit. The first time I put it on I went over to Darlene Pink's house to demonstrate my newfound super outfit. I had every intention of jumping off of her porch to show her how I could fly. But, there was another problem. Darlene had purchased a new Wonder Woman costume and she insisted on jumping first. My first super hero competition turned out to be a bummer. I jumped three different times, but I could never jump as far as Wonder Woman Darlene Pink.

Other than the fact I was vanquished in my first super hero competition, the only other thing I remember about that particular aspiration was I persuaded my mother to fix me a whole can of spinach (a Popeye thing) ... in the hopes it would give me the strength to jump further. All it gave me was diarrhea. To this day I still have trouble with spinach. Or is that more than you wanted to know?

I can't remember what all I aspired to after that. I do recall the time I got interested in becoming a cowboy. I went back to Woolworth's and got a cowboy hat, cowboy chaps, and a cowboy gun. But I was never able to talk my mother into getting me a cowboy horse.

Do you suppose the people taking the survey really want to know all of this?

"It's not the men in my life that count ... it's the life in my men."
Mae West

Any curmudgeon worth his salt knows how to complain. In fact, if you haven't mastered the cynic's art of complaining, grumbling, griping, grousing, and murky murmuring ... when such a response is called for, you probably aren't qualified to call yourself a curmudgeon.

Let me brag a bit. Moonbeam (my bride) will attest to the fact that ... old Karlie is a bona fide curmudgeon; I can fret, repine, moan, groan, second guess, grouch and growl with the best of them. If there is grumbling, complaining, and muttering to be done, you can count on me.

So, when my bride cluttered up my computer with a series of hints on how to alter both my thinking and attitude so that I could get more enjoyment out of life, I figured she was telling me to make some changes.

"What exactly is it you think I ought to do?" I wanted to know. (All certified curmudgeons know this question can only be asked while displaying an annoyed frown.) Frowns imply a certain degree of curmudgeonlyness.

"Slow down," she replied, "and pay attention to your physical and emotional states. In other words, stop and smell the roses."

I did as bride-woman suggested. However, because insects ate all the roses around our domicile, I took a nap instead. Taking a nap may not be "smelling the roses" but it is one of those "slow down your life" tactics I learned from our dog, Freight Train. Freight Train is a real swell sleeper.

I would be remiss if I did not mention that when I awakened from my slumber, I discovered I was still somewhat uncertain about my new lifestyle. To ease any possibility of tension, I took my bride's advice again and took another nap.

"Another thing you should learn to do," Moonbeam pointed out, " ... is learn to reward yourself. Learn to take a break between significant activities."

Actually, this isn't as hard to practice as it sounds. Since lunch and dinner are the two most important activities I undertake during the course of the day, I tried rewarding myself with a four-hour break between the two meals.

Moonbeam was full of advice. "Reserve a block of time each day when you focus on just those things that are of interest to you," she suggested.

I tried to adhere to the routine she suggested. First, I set aside several hours to watch the Chicago Cubs on television. They lost so that didn't work out so well. Then, because I wasn't certain I had set aside enough time to really focus on my interests, I devoted four more hours to my Tuesday night poker game.

After a week of practicing my new, more relaxed and less stressed lifestyle, Moonbeam finally got around to asking me what I thought of it.

"Well, I didn't get very much accomplished," I finally admitted, " ... but I think I do feel something."

"Admit it, didn't you feel stressed before?" she probed.

"Only when you would wake me up to mow the yard or ask me to take out the trash."

"Be honest. Aren't you beginning to see the advantages in inserting those little mini pauses into your schedule? For example, did you try the one where you take a moment to get your thoughts ordered before you pick up the telephone?"

"That one didn't work so well," I confessed. "By the time I got my thoughts ordered, the phone had quit ringing."

"Did you try my suggestion about chewing your food longer and seeing how much more you actually enjoy the taste and texture?" she persisted.

"That doesn't work with Jell-O," I said.

Moonbeam was undaunted. "What about my suggestion to spend more time thinking about what you are eating instead of just wolfing down your food?"

"Who wants to think about vegetables?" I countered. "I can't help it if I think sitting there contemplating the life cycle of the rutabaga is both a little weird and a waste of time."

Moonbeam looked at me and began shaking her head. "You don't want to change, do you? I think you actually enjoy being a curmudgeon."

"Maybe I do," I admitted. "I'm pretty good at it. If I wasn't, I'd go around grinning all the time."

"I seriously doubt it," Moonbeam muttered.

Machismo Is Not An Italian Cheese

"I like men to behave like men. Strong and childish."
Francoise Sagan

Do you chew gum?

I don't. It's not that I really have anything against it. It's just that it has always seemed like it was more trouble than it was worth ... which is another way of saying, I think the reason I never developed a fondness for chomping on Chicklets is due to Sister Arnulfa.

Back in my formative years (read that, my early days in the Catholic grade school system) gum chewing wasn't permitted. In those days a fellow was taking his life in his hands if he ruminated on any gummy substance while in the classroom. Particularly Sister Arnulfa's classroom.

Sister Arnulfa could hear someone slipping a stick of gum between their lips at 50 paces. Then, when the masticating actually started, all (that *word* we weren't allowed to say) broke loose.

"Who's chewing gum?" she would bellow, and the class would freeze in terror. "I hear someone chewing gum," she would shout. When she said that, we would all stop breathing until the culprit revealed himself. I say "himself" because there were never any girls in Sister Arnulfa's class. Even so, Sister always assured us that girls were too smart to chew gum in class. (I don't think so; it's just that girls were smart enough not to get caught.) (They were also smart enough not to be in Sister Arnulfa's class.)

"This class will go no further until I find out who is chewing gum," Sister would thunder. This announcement was always followed by the dreaded mouth inspection. Sister would march up and down the rows of desks, instructing each student to open their mouth so she could conduct her oral audit.

The Curmudgeon Rides Again

If you happened to swallow during the search phase for the guilty party, you were condemned. It may have been circumstantial evidence, but Sister Arnulfa, suspicious soul that she was, was thoroughly convinced no one would dare swallow during the mouth inspection unless they had something to hide.

Melvin Frenk was the biggest (and slowest) kid in our class. Melvin was not only famous for being the only kid in our class that wasn't afraid of Sister Arnulfa, he was also renowned for his world class case of halitosis. Melvin had an award winning case of bad breath. His breath was so bad that if he wanted to play marbles with us at recess, the rest of us guys would just give him our marbles so we didn't have to play with him.

One day we gave Melvin a whole pack of gum and dared him to chew it in class. Melvin, who we were all convinced was braver than Dick Tracy, took the dare. No sooner had Melvin loaded up than Sister Arnulfa heard him chomping.

The world stopped.

"What do you have in your mouth, Melvin?" Sister bellowed.

"Five sticks of peppermint," Melvin acknowledged. (It was actually spearmint, but that's neither here nor there.)

"A whole pack of gum?" Sister said in amazement.

Sins of sins. Melvin was not only breaking the law, he was flaunting it.

"Let me see," Sister demanded.

Melvin opened his mouth and despite the five sticks of spearmint, our fifth grade room was instantly inundated with something akin to poison gas. The student in front of me fainted and Alvin Swit had a choking spell. Through it all, Sister Arnulfa stuck to her guns even though I think she was a bit woozy herself.

Melvin cupped his hand under his mouth and spit out a pinkish glob about the size of a Ping-Pong ball. "Is that what you're looking for?" Melvin wanted to know.

Machismo Is Not An Italian Cheese

"That's disgusting," Sister said. Of course none of us kids thought so. We were at the age though when a Ping-Pong ball sized glob of gum wasn't disgusting ... it was downright funny.

Melvin shook his head. "No, Sister, it ain't disgusting. It's gum."

"Where did you get it?" she screamed.

"The guys gave it to me," Melvin confessed, " ... they dared me to chew it in class."

Sister Arnulfa's face immediately creased into what we all used to call her Hitler look as she slowly surveyed the room of youthful sinners. Then she lowered the boom. "Each of you will have to write 1,000 times, 'I will not encourage Melvin to chew gum in class.'"

Well, we did it, and I was the only one in the room who had to do it over; I misspelled "encourage" 1,000 times.

And you wonder why I have a hang-up about chewing gum?

> "A man, being what he is, is likely to play games that are cruel, devastating, and pitiless. Women, however, are much more genteel. They prefer games that are a combination of larceny, embezzlement and burglary."
> Austin Ellis

Have you ever passed a nodding acquaintance on the street and just automatically (without thinking) asked, "How are you?"

The Curmudgeon Rides Again

Did you really mean to ask that question or did it just sorta pop out because you didn't know what else to say? Did you really care how the person was? Go ahead, rate yourself, on a scale of one to ten. One ... it's a dumb question. Ten ... the milk of human kindness flows in your veins.

Now, after you think about it — were you just trying to be sociable?

I don't know about you, but the responses I get when I ask the question, "How are you?" range all the way from "great" (spoken like a spinster on her first date), to one of those replies that makes you sorry you asked, because the person tells you (down to the last hang nail) about the full spectrum of their physical, mental, and social woes.

Enough already. When will I (or you) learn to quit asking? If you do ask and are frequently sorry you did, when will you quit asking?

Let's be honest. When most folks ask someone they barely know how they are, it's a purely social gesture. It has nothing to do with a search for knowledge or being a caring person. It's small talk. Plain and simple. Nothing more.

Let me give you an example of what I'm talking about. Let's say I pass Uncle Ralph's first wife on the street and experience a fit of social propriety. I say something like, "How are you?" When I do, two things can happen:

(a)   She'll tell me how she is (this may or may not include a lengthy list of miseries real or imagined).

(b)   The lady will tell me she is great.

If she answers (a), the truth is I really didn't want to know and now that I do know, I really don't care. This is known as the *apathy* and *ignorance* approach to socializing. If she answers (b) and informs me she is great, I know she is lying. Uncle Ralph told me she wasn't great a long time ago.

So why did I ask?

Simple. I was trying to be sociable and we (you and I and anyone else guilty of this ill-conceived social habit) waste a lot of time trying to be sociable. Let's be honest, don't you wish you hadn't asked when the person tells you, "My lumbago is bad, my tropical fish all have the ick, and my sister-in-law dumped my younger brother and ran off to Jakarta with a banjo player in a rock band."

O.K. Now you know. More to the point, what are you supposed to say? "Gee, that's too bad." Does that sound trite? Just a bit insincere? If I said that, it sure wouldn't sound sincere.

My point is that no response is appropriate. And if no response is appropriate, why do we ask in the first place? When you stop to think about it, I had several other options besides asking my ill-conceived question. I could have (a) pretended I did not see her, (b) seen her but pretended I did not recognize her, (c) merely nodded and continued on my way. However, if I had resorted to approach (c) she would have accused me of being standoffish ... just as she would have done with approaches (a) and (b). In many cases, it is a lose-lose situation.

By now you're probably thinking I sound like a crotchety old man. Well, if I sound that way it's because I am. I'm tired of trying to be civil and then having to listen to uncivil responses.

Take: *Have a nice day.* What is that supposed to mean? The word "nice" has (by last count) 386 synonyms. Someone could be telling you to have an agreeable day, a refined day, a scrupulous day or a perspicacious day. Hey, if you want someone to have a perspicacious day, say it. Don't beat around the bush with vague terms like "nice."

My bride is one of those indomitable spirits who always

has a cheery greeting or something "nice" to say. She never seems to run out of nice things to say to people. "Drive safely and enjoy the trip." "Don't you just love Indiana and the changing seasons?" "Did you see the beautiful sunset?"

"What's with you?" I say. "Have you looked out the window? There are piles of dirty snow on the ground, it's been raining for two days, the fog has reduced visibility to ten foot in front of the car and I haven't seen the & % * sun for over a week. How the heck am I going to have a "nice" day?"

Our minister, Pastor Good, is just as bad. Last Sunday at the start of the service he looked out the window at the blinding snowstorm and said, "This is the day the Lord has made. Rejoice."

Hey, I've got news for the man in the pulpit, if last Sunday was an example of a day "the Lord has made," the big guy needs practice. As for the "rejoicing" part, I rejoiced all right; the roads were so bad I didn't have to drive to Mongo to watch the Mongo Ballet. I stayed home and watched the ballgame.

Another bit of social drivel is the old "good morning" assessment. My bride does this to me all the time. It's the middle of the night (7 a.m.), the alarm goes off and she chimes in with a merry "good morning." I haven't even had a chance to growl or grumble yet. At seven o'clock in the morning it's too early to tell if it's a "good morning." I haven't even opened my eyes yet. I'm sure as preachin' not ready to make any pronouncements about whether or not it's a good morning. Besides, my idea of a good morning is bacon and eggs, the morning paper, the sunshine glistening off the lake, and a nine o'clock tee time. At seven o'clock in the morning, none of these things have happened yet.

Show business people have the right idea. When they wish someone well, they say, "Break a leg." If that's the case, Moonbeam is destined for stardom; in the last couple of weeks she has had two root canals, broken her arm, hit a deer, and shut her finger in the car door.

When she left the house this morning, I said, "Honey, have a nice day."

She gave me a dirty look.

I guess I should have said, "Have a perspicacious day."

> "A man will tell you that failing to be there when he wants and needs her is a woman's greatest failing, except of course to be there when he doesn't need and want her."
> Helen Rowland

The other morning we were having breakfast with some friends when I went into one of my frequent sneezing fits.

After waiting patiently for me to *achoo* the prescribed ten to twelve times (anything less is called a spasm ... anything over twelve sneezes is called a paroxysm), one of the ladies at the table asked me if I had an allergy.

"Nope," I said rather airily and went on to other matters.

A day or so later, however, I received a pamphlet entitled, "*Tips for Allergy Sufferers*" in the mail. (Reading an occasional pamphlet is about as technical as I get.) It may well be that the well-intentioned person who sent me this little epistle thinks that some of the tips discussed in the pamphlet could alleviate my seemingly unending bouts of sneezing ... or, it could be that the individual is just plain tired of listening to me sneeze.

In either case, here are some of the tips.

The Curmudgeon Rides Again

Tip 1: *Vacuum frequently, particularly your mattress.*

Now I've been sneezing most of my life but this tip about vacuuming the mattress was new to me. It never occurred to me to take the sheets off the bed and run the vacuum sweeper over the mattress. Nevertheless, I tried it. I took off my shoes, got up on the bed and started walking around while I vacuumed. I'm not sure what I accomplished but it was fun. When I realized no one was watching, I jumped up and down ... sorta like a geriatric trampoline. I can't tell that the vacuuming did any good though.

Tip 2: *Use Dacron or foam filled pillows instead of goose down.*

This I'm going to have to check out. I'm a bit skeptical about this one. I don't think geese have anything to do with my sneezing fits. I used to have a pet goose named Hazel when I was 10. I don't remember sneezing when I was around her. Come to think of it, I don't remember seeing her after Christmas that year either.

Tip 3: *Don't have houseplants. If you insist on having houseplants, make certain you keep the leaves clean.*

This tip was disappointing. Why? Because I like houseplants. I have several. My favorite is Boston Fern. I think it's a girl Boston Fern. I call my Boston Fern, Lavinia. If I had called her Fern, her name would have been Boston Fern Fern. That would have been a bit much. At any rate, I looked at how many leaves Lavinia had and decided keeping her leaves clean was too much work.

Tip 4: *Remove "dust collectors" such as rugs, drapes, and stuffed furniture from your room.*

I did this. But you know what? When you do this the room looks rather bare. Plus, there is nowhere to sit down.

Tip 5: *If you are allergic to dogs and cats, remove them from your home.*

Get real.

Our cat's name is *That Damn Cat*. We call her TDC when Pastor Good is around. There is no way I could get rid of her. I've tried. She happened to get locked in my neighbor's garage a couple of weeks ago. He let her out. I'm thinking about shooting him.

As far as TDC is concerned, Moonbeam and I are just a couple of two-legged nuisances. Between 7 and 10 o'clock at night I get to sit in TDC's chair. The rest of the time that chair is off limits to *Homo sapiens*.

As for our dog, Freight Train, Moonbeam has put her foot down. Freight Train isn't allowed to be anyplace except my studio. Moonbeam didn't mind it so much when Freight Train was small, but now that she weighs somewhere in the vicinity of eighty pounds, it's my studio or nothing.

Actually, I don't think I'm allergic to That Damn Cat or Freight Train. But I have noticed that every time my wife gives me a list of things she wants me to do, I start sneezing.

Allergic to a "honey do" list? Gee, what a wonderful possibility.

"It's a scientific fact that if you shave your mustache, you will weaken your eyes."
William Murray
Governor of Oklahoma
1932

More technical stuff.

Moonbeam has an inquiring mind. She is one of those folks who reads "fillers" in newspapers. More to the point, she reads items and then questions whether or not what she has just read is accurate ... or has any significance.

Yesterday we were driving home when she regaled me with the following tidbit. "Did you know," she asked, " ... that American Airlines saved 40,000 by eliminating one olive from every salad they served to in-flight passengers last year?"

Okay all you testosterone motivated male animals out there who like to pretend we know everything, how are we supposed to respond to a bit of information like this?

A)	Should we reveal our ignorance by saying we weren't aware of this fact?

B)	Should we feign interest by saying "really" or "gee, that's interesting?"

C)	Should we actually give some thought to the financial impact on the olive growers of the world?

Let's be honest, I was not mentally agile enough to respond with any of the aforementioned interrogatives, so I gave my bride my standard grunt (which from years of living together means, I heard what you said, I've considered the social significance of the information you just relayed and this grunt is my comment.) But (and this shouldn't surprise anyone who is married) my "better half" wasn't ready to drop the discussion about olives just yet.

"Don't you think that's a lot of money saved for leaving just one olive out of a salad?" Then she adds, "I'm not certain I believe it."

A small confession is in order here. For the record, I rather

Machismo Is Not An Italian Cheese

like olives. I used to buy a bottle of olives, drain the juice off and take my olives to the Wayne Theater on Calhoun Street each Saturday to watch a double feature plus the weekly chapter of *Nyoka, Queen of the Jungle.* Add to that, I have no reason not to believe olive growers are probably wonderful people. Okay?

All of the above notwithstanding, the subject of olives just plain doesn't spark much passion with me. More to the point, I had already turned my feeble, rambling mind to other matters when I heard Moonbeam ask, "How much do you think an olive costs?"

Here we go again. It's a fact. God did not prepare the male species to handle conversations like this. God intended for men to spit, belch, and grunt their way through life. The only articulate response a married man should be expected (or allowed) to make is, "Yes, dear."

"Well," I said, " ... let's see. If an olive costs a penny. That means you could buy 100 olives for one dollar. (See why I included this specific column in the technical section?) That means if American Airlines claims they saved forty thousand dollars, they did not purchase and use 4 million olives last year."

Moonbeam asked me what I thought about that? I told her I thought it was a lot of olives. Then she said, "What do you suppose the olive growers did with the extra four million olives?"

Having no idea what someone would do with an extra four million olives, I gave my bride another of my patented grunts and hoped she would turn her attention to some other world problem. No such luck.

"Where would a person store four million olives?" she asked.

"There is a big ranch for homeless olives in New Mexico," I assured her. "Everything that we, as a society, don't have an immediate use for is stored in New Mexico. That's where we store old airplanes, old rubber bands, and the nation's over-supply of bent darts."

The Curmudgeon Rides Again

· Over the last 40-plus years of our marriage, Moonbeam has learned to disregard my frequently acerbic responses and push on with her concerns. She was at it again. "How many other things do you suppose American Airlines has cut costs on?" she wanted to know.

Do I need to tell you that whatever I was thinking about when Moonbeam unveiled her concern about olives has long since been forgotten? Now, she has me thinking about olives.

"Okay, let me ask you," I said, " ... what would you do about the plight of the olive growers?"

This is a smart move on my part because I am well aware that Moonbeam is the kind of person that has thought about and has answers to questions like this.

"I would start by encouraging people to eat more olives," she said. "Maybe I would pass out recipes that used olives to try to create new markets for olives."

At this point I'm starting to get with the program. "Hey, maybe we could sell them at concession stands in theaters. Or, maybe we could start a trend: peanut butter sandwiches with olives ..."

That's when I realize Moonbeam is looking at me with that old familiar, "Boy, do I wish I had married Arnold Klep" expression.

"Is that the best you can come up with?" she finally asked.

I grunt.

After a long silence, Moonbeam said, "Did you know that the electric chair was invented by a dentist?"

Here we go again.

Irruoptop is Potpourri Spelled Backwards

Potpourri, according to *Webster's Dictionary*, can be dried flower petals, different kinds of herbs, a musical medley, a literary anthology, or as the more literal French translation would have it: *a rotten pot.*

Since that's what this collection of essays (columns, themes, articles, commentaries, discourses, what have you) is, a potpourri ... I have decided to call it an *"irruoptop."*

Why?

Because no one, not even a curmudgeon, wants to think his ramblings belong in a *rotten pot.*

If you haven't already ascertained as much by now, appropriate synonyms for the title "curmudgeon" are such terms as crab, bear, cranky fellow, crosspatch, grouch, boor, grouser, sorehead, bellyacher, churl, yahoo, and a few others that convey much of what has been conveyed in the foregoing.

Am I that bad? My wife thinks so.

However, as a certified "curmudgeon," I cannot help but feel the most important term describing the curmudgeonly state of mind and attitude is *"cynic."* A curmudgeon without an extremely annoying cynical attitude to dominate their thinking (and,

The Curmudgeon Rides Again

in this case, their writing) is not a valid, card carrying curmudgeon.

But, just to make certain you have a thorough concept of the kind of cynicism I'm talking about, let me describe some of the attributes of a true cynic (i.e., curmudgeon). First of all, cynics are pessimists, spreaders of gloom and doom, naysayers, crepehangers, scowlers, grumblers (a gift for "grumbling" is probably my strongest curmudgeonly attribute), complainers, and scoffers. Get the picture?

Let me set the record straight. Being a curmudgeon is not easy. Over the years I have worked long and hard at honing my curmudgeonly abilities. Becoming a difficult, overbearing, ill-humored curmudgeon is much, much harder (I'm not there yet, but I hope to be someday) than folks realize. Displaying spitefulness and acrimony while censuring, sneering, and casting aspersions on others is not as easy as it looks or sounds. It takes practice. It takes dedication.

Why am I telling you all of this? Because, for the next several pages I intend to share my somewhat warped views on everything from report cards, men versus women, gender equity, famous quotes, my mother the Democrat, and much, much more.

I do not expect you to agree with everything I say or suggest (although there is a fellow in Mongo, Indiana, who claims I have never led him wrong ... I visit him at the Carsonaire State Mental Institution in Orland at least once a month).

Truth be known, the only people who will read and enjoy the ramblings that follow are the kinds of individuals who peek around corners to make certain they won't run into someone or something they like and be forced to make small talk.

To put you in the proper frame of mind for dealing with what follows, I would like to share this thought from Robert B. Parker with you:

"Fourteen years in the professor dodge has taught me that one can argue ingeniously on behalf of any theory applied to any piece of literature. This is rarely harmful, because normally no-one reads such essays."

Or, perhaps this will even better explain why I am a cynic:

A year or so after *The Prometheus Project* (my third novel) was released, I was invited to hear a discussion and critique of the work by a prestigious women's literary group in Indianapolis.

But there was a hitch. I was to sit in the back of the room and the women who were doing the critiquing were not told that I was present.

What I heard was a discussion of a book that in no way even faintly resembled anything I had written. One woman said that one certain passage was doubtless intended to be "a metaphor for life." Another claimed she could read between the lines and that my "soul was crying out in anguish."

Later, when I was called to the podium, the panel moderator asked me why I had written the book. I told them to guess. Not one single reader was able to nail down the real reason.

"Hey," I said, " ... it's real simple. I got paid for it."

The Curmudgeon Rides Again

"Women want mediocre men, but men are having difficulty reaching that lofty level."
Torry Marks
1977

It's Mother's Day. I think I'll give Mom a call and see how she is enjoying her special day.

RING-RING RING-RING RING-RING (It takes Mom awhile to get to the phone.)

"Hi, Mom, Happy Mother's Day."

SILENCE

"I said, 'Happy Mother's Day, Mom.' Did you get the flowers?"

"Is this Karl, my only son, the one who broke his mother's heart by voting for George Bush?"

"Yeah, Mom, it's me, your Republican voting son. How are you?"

"Better you should ask Mrs. Lincoln how she enjoyed the play. Better you should have been born on April 1 because you are such a fool. What has God got against me? He gives me one son to warm my heart and the same son breaks it by turning out to be a Republican."

"I keep telling you, Mom, I am not a Republican. I'm an Independent. This time I voted Republican because I was convinced Bush was the best man for the job. As it turns out I was right. Look how he handled the Desert Storm situation."

HARUMPH. "Only because he was getting advice from General Schwarzkopf, a very good Democrat. I have it on very good authority that every one of those brave boys that went over there to fight was a registered Democrat."

"Can we talk about something else besides politics, Mom?"

"No, we can't. Now your uncle tells me that you are writing a column for a paper call *Herald-Republican*. How could you? When you were young I told your Uncle Truman that you were the kind of boy who would someday break your mother's heart. I can't bring myself to say it ... (cough-choke) ... working for a Republican newspaper."

"Since you seem to be determined to talk politics, Mom, what did you think of the latest Kennedy fiasco down in Florida?"

"Lies and scandal-mongering; that's all it is. Republican inspired. A Kennedy would never do such a thing. I don't believe that anymore than I believe all that tripe about John and Robert and Marilyn Monroe. There is no doubt in my mind that it was a Republican newspaper that dug up that smut just to smear the Kennedy name."

"Speaking of scandal-mongering, have you read Kitty Kelley's book about Nancy Reagan?"

"The woman is a saint," Mom extolled.

"Mrs. Reagan?"

"Of course not. I'm talking about Kitty Kelly ... such an honest, truthful, hard-working girl."

"Don't tell me you actually believe all that stuff she wrote about our former First Lady?"

"Of course it's true. Wasn't that Reagan woman a former actress? Isn't she married to a Republican? Doesn't she hang around with all those show business people? Doesn't she ride horses? If she was an honest, hardworking woman, she wouldn't have time for all that nonsense. Republicans have a reputation for doing those kinds of things. Look at Nixon. No self-respecting Democrat would have authorized a break-in like Nixon did at Potter's Gate."

"That's Watergate, Mom."

"Whatever. My point is America's First Lady should be more like Barbara Bush."

"Barbara Bush is a Republican, Mom."

SILENCE

"I said, 'Barbara Bush is a Republican,' Mom."

"Did I say Barbara Bush? I mean Eleanor Roosevelt. Now there was a First Lady the whole nation could look up to."

"Why? How tall was she?"

"Show respect," Mom scolded.

"Well, I really didn't call to discuss politics, Mom. I just called to say Happy Mother's Day and to see how you were feeling."

"I'd feel just fine if we could get this country back on the right track ... and the only way to do that is elect ourselves a Democrat president."

"Okay, Mom. Whatever you say. By the way, everyone here sends their love and says to wish you a Happy Mother's Day for them."

HANG UP ... go back into the living room. Long time bride looks up from her latest self-help book and smiles. "How was your mother, dear?"

"Miserable. At least until the next election."

"Authors are easy to get along with ... if you enjoy children."
Michael Joseph
London Observer

I have respect for some of my relatives. The operative word though is *"some."* For the most part, my bride's family is

Irruoptop is Potpourri Spelled Backwards

cool. Same goes for my family. On the other hand, we do have a few tribal connections to fugitives from the land of *non compos mentis*. Take, for example, my wife's Uncle Darrel.

He stopped by the other day. Now the truth is, we don't see Uncle Dud (that's what the kids call him) very much. Why? Because Uncle Dud moves in his own strange little circle. In fact, he is known, far and wide, as a myth postulator. My oldest son, Trump West, has a different name for him; he calls him Uncle Prevaricator. Are you getting a picture? On the other hand, Uncle Dud's wife claims he once received an award for being the most gullible person at a liar's convention. As you can see, our tribe isn't real sure where Uncle Dud falls on the old veracity scale.

I guess the best way of explaining it is – to Uncle Dud there is no such thing as fantasy, whimsy or implausibility. He believes everything you tell him and he repeats what he hears as the gospel truth.

Let me give you an example. I remember the time Uncle Dud heard that if you stand on the corner of Hollywood and Vine (you know where that is) long enough, eventually you will see most of the big movie personalities in Tinsel Town.

"Is it true?" I asked him.

"Probably," he said, " ... but I don't think I got a real good shot at it. I wasn't there long enough. I had only been standing there a couple of weeks when I got arrested for vagrancy."

After hearing that, you'll probably agree with me ... good old Uncle Dud isn't exactly a candidate for the war room of a think tank. Take the time he was telling me someone told him, "If you put tin foil inside your hubcaps, it confuses police radar."

"I don't think so," I told him. "That sounds like an old wives' tale to me."

Uncle Dud shook his head and assured me he hadn't heard from any of the old wives he knew. "Actually," he told me, " ... my neighbor is the one that told me about it and his name is Gus."

Then he added, "Gus is a guy."

Aunt Tinker (Uncle Dud's wife) later revealed Uncle Dud had been ticketed for speeding while trying to demonstrate the tin foil in the hubcap deception to one of his friends. That friend was Gerald Miller, a twenty-seven-year veteran of the Golnern police department.

I still remember the time we were discussing weather. "I suppose," he said, " ... you've heard the concern about global warming? Not only that, now scientists are claiming we are on the verge of another ice age."

"Wait a minute," I laughed, " ... one or the other is possible. Not both. If you have global warming, you can't have an ice age at the same time."

Uncle Dud gave me that look that elders like to bestow on younger folks. You know ... it says you are totally incapable of handling some of the larger-than-life concepts that older (and obviously wiser) folks have to deal with.

"Of course, you can have both," Uncle Dud declared. "The hole in the ozone layer is closer to the South Pole. Right? That's what's lettin' all the heat in and that's where we're gettin' all that global warming stuff. Got it?"

I nodded. I figured he was going somewhere with his hypothesis; I wanted to know where.

"The ice age is a whole different matter. It comes from the north where all the icebergs are."

"But there are icebergs at the South Pole too," I reminded him.

That's when I received another "boy are you dumber than dirt" look from good, old Uncle Dud. "Which way is south?" he wanted to know.

"Well," I said, " ... if you were looking at a wall map, north is up, south is down, and ..."

Uncle Dud cut me off before I could finish. "Duh," he

said, "... have you ever known of an iceberg to break off from the South Pole ice cap, start flowin' north and sink a ship like the *Titanic*?"

"No," I admitted.

"Well," he explained, "that's because icebergs from the South Pole don't come north; they just fall off the earth down there and tumble off into space. Then along comes a strong wind and they become part of a gigantic ice storm. Hence ... the ice age returns."

Over the years I've learned that very little can be accomplished by arguing with Uncle Dud. I usually just try to steer him toward another subject. But one time I said, "Unc, I'm curious, where do you get these weird ideas?"

He looked at me. "I suppose you're one of them folks who thinks you can break a mirror and not have seven years of bad luck," he said.

"Wait a minute," I said, "I don't *think* breaking mirrors is bad luck. I *know* it is. When you break one you have to go spend a wad of money on a new one. I call that bad luck."

It was later that same night, as Moonbeam and I, along with Uncle Dud, were sitting down at the dinner table, that the old boy started laughing.

"What's so funny, Uncle Dud?" my bride asked.

Uncle Dud leaned toward my bride and lowered his voice. "I gotta tell you, girl," he chuckled. "You know what that klutz husband of yours thinks? He actually thinks he's gonna have bad luck if he breaks a mirror."

The Curmudgeon Rides Again

"If you can't say anything good about someone, come over here and sit by me." Alice Roosevelt Longworth

Do you use the word "cool" to describe something neat? Many people do.

Truth is, I use it all the time. I even use it when I should probably take a moment and search for a better term to describe how I feel about something. With me the word "cool" is a habit. I have been using the word "cool" since I was in high school.

That's a long time. (Read that "really long time.")

Truth be known, I probably should have discarded the habit a long time ago. I know more words than that. Besides, it probably sounds "uncool" for a man my age to go around using a slang expression from his high school days.

The word "cool" belongs to a younger generation. By younger generation I mean anyone younger than me. That includes a lot of people. In fact, it includes almost all the people. Nevertheless, it seems to me people should be able to use the word "cool" to describe whatever it is they are describing until they think they are too old to be using it. Does that make sense? It probably makes as much sense as using the word "cool" to describe something "hot."

I don't know why I thought it was cool to use the word "cool." If you look up the word "cool" in the dictionary you will discover it has several definitions. The majority of those definitions relate to temperature. A cool temperature isn't the "cool" I'm referring to though. The "cool" I'm talking about has to do with a degree of excellence or how much an individual admires a certain something. Don't ask me why I don't say "excellent" instead of "cool." When I began using the term I was a teenager...

and who can explain why teenagers do what they do?

The word "cool" isn't a gender thing. It isn't reserved for the exclusive use of men. If it was, women would say it was sexist and men wouldn't be allowed to use it.

Strangely enough, "cool" can be used to describe "hot." If it's "really hot" ... it can be "really cool." Understand? Note, however, that the "really hot" in this case has nothing to do with temperature. "Really hot" when you are referring to temperature is more closely associated with terms like "sweltering" or "oven-like." But, when a man says a woman is "cool" he is probably referring to someone very attractive. When a man says a woman is "really cool" he is referring to someone like Sharon Stone which, in this particular case, is "really hot" as in "unholy smoke."

On the other hand, "cool" isn't "cold." If it's "cold" it is something other than "cool."

The word "cool" has a bunch of synonyms. Most of which have nothing to do with the way those of us who use the word "cool" describe the aforementioned degree of excellence. While "cool" doesn't refer to nippy or unheated, it may, in an oblique fashion, refer to being "composed" or "relaxed." But, it has nothing to do with being "unfriendly" or "distant."

"Cool" is the root word for the oft used term "cool it." (which means "take it easy"). The dictionary describes that as slang. However, if you say "cool off," that isn't slang ... that's called informal English. "Cool off" is the root derivation of "chill out" which has nothing to do with what we are talking about here ... but I thought you would like to know that.

While "cool" means "good" or "neat" to those of us who use the term to describe degree of worth, fineness, or quality, it is not a term we would use to describe good food ... except, of course, in the aforementioned oblique form. If you want "hot" food and it's cool, that's not "cool." But if you order hot food (pizza, for instance), and it's hot when you get it, that's "cool."

The Curmudgeon Rides Again

When you are driving down Interstate 69 and approach Fairmount, Indiana, you will see signs that describe James Dean as the epitome of "cool." I'll go along with that. James Dean was cool all right. Afterall, he drove a Porsche and a Porsche is a "cool" car.

Having said all that I still don't think James Dean is as "cool" as Sharon Stone.

> ## "It is said that there is one woman whom fate has destined for each of us. If that is true, I have missed mine ... three times."
> ### attributed to Lawrence King

Moonbeam and I are on different schedules and sometimes that causes problems. By the time I take our dog, Freight Train, out for her morning constitutional, take a shower, and get ready for the day's activities, Moonbeam has jumped into her Momserati and ventured off to the school wars where she is school nurse. Before departing, however, my long-time bride sometimes leaves me notes. Yesterday she left me with this gem:

> *"The latter part*
> *of a wise man's life*
> *is taken in curing*
> *the follies, prejudices,*
> *and false opinions*
> *he had contracted*
> *in the former."*

Hey, after 40 years of marriage, I can hardly be called a

Irruoptop is Potpourri Spelled Backwards

rookie in this wife-husband communication thing (read that: normally I know what Moonbeam is getting at). This one, however, left me with a whole bunch of questions and no wife to enlighten me.

Did she think some of my "ventures" were "folly?" Was she finally revealing her true feelings about the time I bought the semi-load of watermelons without knowing what I was going to do with them? If that's the case, I don't think she understands what a deal I thought I was getting when I drove up to that overturned semi and the driver offered (well, he said he was the driver) to sell me every watermelon on that truck for a buck a piece. I still don't think the Sheriff would have had to charge me with unlawful possession of watermelon(s). He's not the one who lost seven hundred bucks on the deal. Plus court costs.

And what about this "prejudice" accusation?

I don't think anyone who is willing to sit down and break bread every Thanksgiving with my wife's Uncle Ralph can be called prejudiced. I mean if you want to see tolerance with a capital "T", you ought to see how hard I work trying to have a conversation with that creature from the cartoon pages. I haven't shown that much patience and forbearance since I tried to get the Internal Revenue Service auditor to understand why I wanted to write off my trips out to the Angola Motor Speedway. He wasn't buying it when I told him I wanted to do a book on racing.

The thing that really rankles me though is the "false opinion" bit.

Was she telling me there was a wrinkle in my reasoning? Was she telling me I arrived at too many false conclusions? Was she accusing me of brain cramps? Was she referring to the time I dressed up like Frankenstein and stiff-legged my way onto the night shift at the retirement home?

I thought it was funny. How was I to know those nurses would scream and holler like that? Is it my fault all that yelling and commotion woke up the residents? Is it my fault they had to change all those sheets?

I apologized. I didn't know nurses knew that kind of language. I've been meaning to look up some of those words.

At any rate, when Moonbeam came home the night I found her message, I met her at the door. I was armed and ready. Why wouldn't I be? I had been fretting all day.

"So you think some of my business ventures are nothing more than folly," I growled.

Moonbeam looked at me.

"And what's this about being prejudiced?" I wanted to know.

My bride feigned not knowing what I was talking about (like most women she is very skilled at giving me questioning looks).

"And this last one ... the one about me having 'false opinions' really frosts me," I informed her. By this time my face was red and puffy. I hate that. I don't look good in "red" and "puffy."

Bride-woman cleared her throat. "I don't have the slightest idea what you're talking about," she said.

"This," I said. I held out the piece of paper with her unkind observations about my supposed frailties. "This note you left me. I found it laying on the table."

"Oh, that," she said. "I'm glad you found it. I thought I had lost it."

"I'll just bet you're glad I found it," I snarled.

"I was supposed to take it to school with me. It's a quote from Jonathan Swift. One of the teachers at school wants me to do it in calligraphy."

"I knew that," I said.

Irruoptop is Potpourri Spelled Backwards

"When my cousin, Jerome, visits, I derive great pleasure. That pleasure comes from knowing that, generally speaking, it will be quite some time before his next visit."
Helen Turner
Relatives

Some time back I went to one of those self-help seminars that are supposed to teach you how to better yourself and enhance the quality of your life.

Ever been to a self-help seminar?

This particular seminar had an intrinsic appeal to me. It was all about how to save time. I need a seminar devoted to "how to save time." I always said if I could find the time, I would go to one of those time saving seminars.

On a scale of one to ten, with one being the lowest score possible, I would rate this seminar as a five. Five is average. Why would I rate it as only a five? Because while a number of the time-saving recommendations were okay, I don't think they were very well thought out. I'll show you what I mean.

Suggestion 1. Keep an appointment calendar by the phone.

This didn't save me any time at all. I spent as much time looking for something to write with as I used to spend looking for the calendar. The suggestion should have been more explicit. It should have mentioned having something to write with too.

Suggestion 2. Keep a notebook in the car's glove compartment so you can jot down ideas when you are driving.

This isn't real handy either. The other day I had an idea

The Curmudgeon Rides Again

and I wasn't in the car.

Suggestion 3. Put things away after you are finished using them.
    This one sounds good on the surface ... but I have to ask, how do you know when you are done with them? If I need them sometime next week, I'll just have to go to all the trouble of getting them out again.

Suggestion 4. Lay out the next day's clothes before you go to bed at night.
    Obviously this person never lived in Indiana. The weather changes fast around these parts. We can't be certain how we should be dressed three hours from now. Certainly not tomorrow morning.

Suggestion 5. Have your checks mailed directly to your account at your bank.
    Checks?

Suggestion 6. Hire a neighborhood teenager to do your yard work.
    Teenager? Work?

Suggestion 7. Know when you have reached peak efficiency. When you do, stop and refresh yourself. Enjoy the accomplishment.
    Okay, efficiency fans, this one works. When I wake up in the morning, I know that is as efficient as I am going to get that day. So, I follow the suggestion; I lay in bed until this feeling of peak efficiency passes. That's when I take my first nap of the day.

Suggestion 8. Avoid negative people who have a "can't do" approach to things.
    This one is really tough. Everywhere I go, there I am.

Irruoptop is Potpourri Spelled Backwards

Suggestion 9. Spend 10 minutes a day exercising. Stretch frequently.

This is another one that, on the surface, looks as though it might work. But, if you exercise for ten minutes, you are going to be worn out. I know, I tried it once. It's been my experience that if one exercises for ten minutes, it takes a good half-hour to recuperate.

Suggestion 10. Cut down on gossip, trivial conversations and unrewarding television watching.

See what I mean about some of these suggestions not being realistic? How is a person expected to know what is going on in his community if that person doesn't gossip? No trivial conversations? Hey, get real. I'm a man. Besides, watching ESPN is not trivial.

Suggestion 11. Make a list of things a person can accomplish in five minutes.

This list is going to vary for practically everyone. Example: A bald headed guy could get a haircut in five minutes. Three-minute eggs? I don't think so. It would take me the full five minutes just to figure out how to turn on the stove.

Suggestion 12. Tape a list of the things you need when you travel inside your suitcase.

The only time I travel is when wife-woman throws me out of the house. When that happens she usually doesn't give me time to pack a suitcase.

Suggestion 13. When you throw something away, practice wastebasket basketball.

This one, I have to admit, is cool in concept. I tried it. I wadded up several pieces of paper and tried to make "baskets" with them. I missed one hundred and thirty-seven times in a row. Then I had to get up and go over and pick up one hundred and thirty-seven wads of paper.

This may be a time saver for Michael Jordan, but not me.

Suggestion 14. Have an automatic reply for telemarketing calls.
This one is a piece of cake, "Go away."

Suggestion 15. Buy two books of stamps at the same time and save a trip to the post office.
I can't. My wife won't let me carry that much money at one time. Even if she did let me have enough to buy two books of stamps ... they would probably raise the price of stamps before I had used all the stamps in those two books. Then I would have to go back to the post office anyway.

Suggestion 16. Don't even bother to read junk mail. Walk straight to the basket and throw it away.
Junk mail is the only kind I get and I can't open it?

"God is not dead.
He is alive and this time he is working on
a much less ambitious project."
graffiti

A friend of mine sent me a list of her social club's favorite things. I read the list, thought about it, and after much cogitation on the matter, feel compelled to confess that some of the "favor-

Irruoptop is Potpourri Spelled Backwards

ite things" on my friend's list wouldn't be on mine.

The only concession I will make is, some of the differences are the result of gender. Others are just plain due to the fact that this woman and her sisterhood club members are a bunch of sunny optimists, which, if you read this column from time to time, you know I'm not.

At any rate, here is their list of favorite things.

1. Watching sunrises.

Come on. Watching sunrises? No way. The minute the sun peeps over the horizon I've got an eighty-pound dog standing beside the bed waiting for me to take her for a walk. That's pressure. I don't need pressure like that so early in the morning.

Hey, for those it hasn't occurred to, "sunrise" means night is over. That means it's time to get up. It also means I am all through doing for that day what I do best. The way I look at it, it's all downhill after sunrise.

2. Making chocolate chip cookies.

This is a pet peeve of mine. What's with this chocolate chip thing? Where is it written that all cookies have to be made with chocolate chips? What's wrong with plain old oatmeal or peanut butter cookies? Why is it you cookie makers have to put chocolate chips in everything?

I'll tell you what I think. I think people put chocolate chips in everything to cover up the mistakes they make putting the rest of the cookie recipe together.

3. Cuddled up on the couch with a loved one watching one of our favorite movies.

Sure, I get to do that ... as long as I'm willing to watch huggy kissy movies. I don't like the kind of movies Moonbeam likes.

Moonbeam doesn't like the kind of movies I like. My three favorite movies are *Truckstop Girls On The Moon*, *Godzilla Eats Miami*, and *The Curse of the Really Big Mushrooms*. Moonbeam doesn't care for any of them.

Sometimes I have Freight Train watch my favorite movies with me. But you can't cuddle with her. She smells bad.

4. *Hot chocolate.*

I'll have to admit it. This would be one of my favorite things too ... if hot chocolate didn't give me gas.

5. *Having someone play with your hair.*

I thought this sounded like fun, so I let my grandson play with his electric train in my hair. My hair got all tangled up in the wheels of his engine and I got a shock. It is not as much fun as it sounds.

6. *Romantic midnight phone calls.*

Okay, let's face it. These chicks are way out weird. Right? When I read this one I came to the realization that the disparity between men and women is even greater than I thought.

In my opinion, you have to be slightly deranged to like phone calls at midnight. Think about it. It's midnight. The phone rings. You stumble out of bed. You pick up the receiver. You say, "Hello." What happens? The clown on the other end of the line realizes he has dialed the wrong number and refuses to apologize or even talk. Bottom line, you stand there with the receiver in your hand. Where's the romance in that little scenario?

If that isn't what happens, you get a good dose of nasty news. Uncle Belcher has run off with his French housekeeper and your Aunt Prune (whom you can't stand) is coming to live with you until she gets over the trauma.

So what do you do? In either case you go back to bed and lay there ... wide awake. Guess who can't sleep?

7. Getting mail.

Did I ever tell you about the analysis I did on the mail delivered to the Curmudgeon digs over one seven-day period? Exactly one half of the fifty-six pieces of mail received during the week were advertisements for things neither bride-woman nor I purchased, needed, or wanted. Several of the remaining pieces of mail offered us either "opportunities to buy at bargain prices," or additional information about replacement windows, aluminum siding, a fine new catalog from Victoria's Secret, two new government publications, a 20% discount on lawn care services, and a rather intriguing offer from The Hair Club for Men.

In addition we were notified that we were "preapproved" for "new, lower rate" credit cards from four different banks. The vet sent us a card for Freight Train's annual check up. Moonbeam received two letters. And I got a notice to appear for jury duty. So much for mail.

8. A special glance.

I've only done this "special glance" thing a handful of times in my whole life. Most of them were unintended. Admittedly, I'm not very good at it. Marlene Bigg misinterpreted my "special glance" when I was in the sixth grade. She hit me with her gym bag and I got a black eye. The other "special glance" that I remember was at the Fort Wayne auto auction. They said I boughta Nash Rambler.

9. A hot shower.

Finally a "favorite thing" I could agree with. In fact, that's where I'm headed now ... as soon as I have adequately explained to Moonbeam about that "special glance" I gave Marlene Bigg back in the sixth grade.

> "The urge to gamble is so universal,
> and its practice so pleasurable,
> it's only natural to assume it is immoral."
> Haywood Broun

Moonbeam and I were out for a drive the other day when we saw two fellows standing in a yard looking at a lawn mower. The lawn mower wasn't running and the men were standing there, scratching their heads, spittin', talkin' and wearin' slightly perplexed expressions.

"What are they doing?" Moonbeam wanted to know.

"Fixing the lawnmower," I informed her.

Some distance down the road, we saw an open manhole cover. Three men were standing there, staring down the hole, looking slightly bewildered.

"And what are they doing?" Moonbeam asked.

"Well," I said, displaying my immediate grasp of the maleness in what was, in all probability, a sewer type technical problem, " ... they are discussing how to correct whatever problem caused them to open the manhole cover in the first place."

Moonbeam acknowledged my response to her query with a polite smile.

Still later, on the outskirts of Mongo, we saw two men putting up fence. When we passed, they were standing, one with arms folded, the other, leaning on a shovel, assessing how effectively they had erected a corner post.

Bride-woman looked at them and then me. "I suppose

you are going to tell me that those guys are working too," she said.

"Were they standing and talking?" I asked.

She nodded.

"Did they have baffled looks on their faces?" I asked.

Moonbeam continued to nod.

"Were they spittin'?"

"They were spitting," she confirmed.

"Then they were working," I assured her. "Haven't you ever noticed, when men are solving problems, especially work related problems, they stand around, do a lot of talking, scratch their heads, and do a lot of spitting."

"Why?" my bride pressed. "Women don't spit when they work. Why do men feel the necessity to spit?"

"It's a guy thing," I assured her. "If two men are working on a problem and one of them isn't spitting, the other fellow knows his partner isn't working very hard to get the job done."

Moonbeam shook her head. "I don't see you spit very often," she said.

"That just proves my point. A) I don't spit because I don't generally have work problems. B) I don't spit because I don't have to prove I'm working to some other guy. C) I don't do a whole lot of work."

"Who teaches men to spit in the first place?" she wanted to know.

"Our fathers teach us," I said. "You know that old saying, 'Like father, like son?' Well, they start by teaching us to stand around and stare at a lawnmower. Actually, though, when I was the age when my father was first starting to teach me to stare, we were too poor to own a lawnmower. So I learned to stand and stare by watching our goat, Mabel, eat grass. That's also when we men learn to stand with our arms folded. That's called the 'thinkin' about the problem stance.' When we've mastered those

The Curmudgeon Rides Again

work habits, our fathers teach us how to send someone back up to the house to fetch a screwdriver or pair of pliers. We don't have any idea what we're gonna do with the screwdriver or pliers, but it makes people think we know how to fix whatever's wrong."

"Fetch?" Moonbeam repeated.

"Cool word, huh? It means ..."

"I know what it means," she cut me off. "Surely you can't be serious about all of this."

"I sure am serious. How do you think us guys all learn to act this way? It's part of the universal brotherhood. Sort of like instinct. A father passes it down to his son, a son passes it on to his son, and .... I've got a grandson in California who never had to put in any fence like his father but I'll bet he knows how to spit and stare at work."

"Okay, what about that spitting? When do you learn to do that?"

"Spitting comes last. A good father doesn't teach his son to spit until he's learned to send other people after tools, lean on a shovel, look down a hole, scratch his head, discuss different ways of fixing things, get a cup of coffee, go to the bathroom, and three ways to fix most things with duct tape. When the boy learns all those, then he's earned the right to spit."

At that point Moonbeam looked around. There was a somewhat concerned look on her face. "I think we're lost," she said. "Maybe you better ask someone for directions."

"No way," I said. "That's another man thing. Men never admit they are lost."

"After being married to you all these years," she said, "I knew that."

My Favorite Holiday Hasn't Been Invented Yet

"I like to reflect back on my parents' wedding day. It was quite an occasion. Quite a party. My father was twenty. My mother was nineteen. I was three."
Billie Holiday

Around our humble palace of inhabitancy there is a perpetuating and often annoying enthusiasm for certain holidays that involve assembling the tribe to eat and drink. This happens most often on Christmas, Thanksgiving, Reunion Day (a floating holiday), and Mother's Day. Other holidays, such as Easter, Cat Lover's Day, and Be Kind to Bullfrogs Day, all tend to inspire much less excitement, fervency, and zeal.

You may have noticed that I did not mention Father's Day. On Father's Day, I can count on one card and phone calls from the other four progeny. The callers on Father's Day usually say something like, "Hi, Dad, is Mom there?"

Why is this, I ask myself? Despite their congenial salutation (i.e., "Dad") which, on the surface at least, would seem to acknowledge my role in their presence on this old planet, they seem to be in a state of denial.

The Curmudgeon Rides Again

Are they denying I am their father?

Is there some sort of suppressed resentment or acrimony present ... because they are aware I am blissfully spending their inheritance in a fit of geriatric debauchery?

Whatever.

Let's set the record straight. For the most part, I am opposed to many of our holidays. The holidays we do celebrate have been prostituted. How? On Memorial Day we do less and less memorializing. On Labor Day we work hard at saying goodbye to summer. On Thanksgiving we worry about how much we're going to eat ... and on Christmas, we are more concerned about making certain we didn't overlook or overspend for those names on our gift list.

"What's wrong with that?" you say.

Well, I'm no moralist, but I am saying the holidays we do get around to celebrating we seem to be celebrating in the wrong fashion for the wrong reason. Then, on top of that, I'm saying there are any number of holidays we should be celebrating but are being overlooked.

Let me give you an example of what I mean. Do you like to be clean? Do you like to smell clean? Most of us do ... so why don't we celebrate National Soap Day? Everyone could dress up like a bar of their favorite soap on National Soap Day. There would be prizes for the person who looked (and smelled) the most like a bar of *Dove* or *Irish Spring* or whatever that person's soap preference is.

Instead of Ground Hog Day (which isn't all that important now that we get long range forecasting from the Weather Bureau), we could have Pet Melon Day. Kids could bring their pet watermelon, or cantaloupe, or honey dew melon to school for a bring and brag session. (Yes, the melon would have to be on a leash.) The child then with the best-trained melon would receive a prize and both the melon and child would be interviewed on television on the local six o'clock news.

My Favorite Holiday Hasn't Been Invented Yet

Or, how about Wash a Tombstone Day. How many of us drive by cemeteries every day, completely unaware of how much our dearly departed and their tombstones need attention? A little soap, a little water, a little elbow grease, and a few plastic flowers could make the aforementioned dearly departed proud of their surroundings.

On Wash a Tombstone Day, folks would rise early, gather their cleaning utensils and march to the nearest cemetery. Rub. Scrub. Clean. Brush. Cleanse. Polish. Then, because of you and people like you, America would become known as the *Land of Clean Boneyards*. Sorta makes you proud just thinking about it. Doesn't it?

On balance, I personally don't think we have enough holidays. In Europe, whole countries, cities, towns, villages close down for holidays. I think we should do likewise here ... but for the right reason. Perhaps the IRS could arrange for all income tax refunds to be received by recipients on the same day. Think what that could be like. Millions upon millions upon millions of tax wielding American shoppers attacking the shopping malls of America in an orgy of inventory depleting spending. Traffic gridlock, entire computer banking systems breaking down, credit cards melting in the heat of a purchasing frenzy. Wow. What a holiday. Makes President's Day seem a little tame, doesn't it?

The Curmudgeon Rides Again

> "The reason some men continue to smile when everything starts to go wrong is because they have already figured out who they are going to blame it on."
>
> *Jones' Law*
> A. Bloch

Talk about special days. Remember report card day?

Fortunately, I had almost forgotten about report cards until we went to visit a friend the other night. We hadn't much more than relieved ourselves of our coats when the man of the house began extolling the academic achievement of his granddaughter.

"Look at this," he crowed. "A in reading. A in spelling. A in arithmetic. A in everything. The kid is a genius. Her teachers as much as told me she is the smartest kid they ever had in their classes."

Moments later, when little Prunells made her grand entrance, she dutifully recited the alphabet, multiplication tables through five, and rattled off a couple of poems.

"Pretty good for a five year old, huh?" her grandfather preened. "Makes me look forward to report card time because I know I'm going to see all A's."

Truth be known, I never thought report card time was that big of a deal. In fact, I rather dreaded the whole 12-week reporting system.

Back at Saint Crazy House, Monsignor Moose used to stride over from the parish house once every academic quarter to pass out report cards. Monsignor used to sit at the desk in the front of the classroom, rummage through the cards until he found one with lots of red marks on it and then call out the student's name.

My Favorite Holiday Hasn't Been Invented Yet

Mine was usually the first name he would call.

"Karl. Karl Lagrent," he would thunder.

"That's Largent, Monsignor," I tried to point out, " ... the 'r' comes before the 'g.'"

"Whatever," Monsignor would mutter. "Look at all the red marks. This report card looks like it's having a severe hemorrhage."

"That's not blood, Monsignor," I stammered. "That's red ink. Sister Mankiller likes red ink."

The way Monsignor was shaking his head. I figured this was as good a time as any for the world to come to an end. "It says here," he growled, " ... that you received a check mark in deportment."

"I don't know how that could have happened, Monsignor," I said, " ... we haven't studied deportment yet." Then because I was feeling pretty sure of myself, I informed him that we didn't study deportment until after we finished studying fractions.

"It says here that you giggle and talk in class," he grunted.

I tried to explain to Monsignor that when Arnold Flit would stick an empty olive bottle in his mouth, slap himself on the back of the head, and catapult his glass missile across the room at Lucy Plimp when Sister wasn't looking, I just naturally got the giggles. Monsignor quickly rummaged through the deck of report cards, found the one belonging to Arnold Flit and point out that Arnold didn't have "giggles and talks in class" noted on his card.

"That's because Sister never sees him do it," I tried to explain.

Monsignor wasn't about to let me up. "What's this red mark in attendance?" he wanted to know. "According to your report card, you missed one day of school."

"My goldfish died," I tried to explain. "It was really sad, Monsignor. I came home from school and there he was, floating on his side."

The Curmudgeon Rides Again

"A dead goldfish is no justification for missing school," Monsignor thundered. "What would you do if someone really important died?"

I told him I'd probably take more than one day off.

It was a ritual. Monsignor would always scowl at me, look down at my card, shake his head, and then look up again. Some times when there was lots of red on my card he would repeat the routine several times. But no matter how many times he looked up at me and back down at the card, he would always conclude his little ceremony by saying, "What are we going to do with you, Lagrent?"

"That's Largent, Monsignor. In Largent the 'r' comes before the 'g.'"

When Monsignor said, "Whatever," I knew we were going to go through the same ritual again, twelve weeks from now ... unless ... unless I could hide Sister Mankiller's red pen.

"Guaranteed. If it's good, they'll stop making it." Political cartoonist, Herbert Block (Herblock)

Under normal circumstances, when Moonbeam decides to give a party, she is the one who plans everything down to the last detail. I usually don't get involved. To my way of thinking, Reunion Day at our house is every bit as big as Paint Your Portable Outhouse Day for the rest of the nation.

Just for the record, let me say that I'm not exactly certain you can call a "family reunion" a holiday, but there are a lot of other things you can call it. Nevertheless, the preparations are

My Favorite Holiday Hasn't Been Invented Yet

about the same. Ergo, my bride-woman has been doing a lot of planning lately and for some strange reason she has asked me to get involved this year.

But, all this won't mean much to you if I don't regale you with a little background. Several years ago, Moonbeam, who comes from a large family, decided it would be a good idea to have our own family reunion. Not only did she decide to have a family reunion, she decided to have an "annual" family reunion. She also decided it would be scheduled on Saturday of the first weekend in July. Last year we celebrated (that's her word for it, not mine) our tenth reunion.

Most of these shindigs have run fairly smooth. But back in 1996 we were confronted with our first real problem. Moonbeam had to move her eating orgy back (or was it forward?) a week. No big deal, you say, a handful of semi rational adult members of the clan ought to be able to accommodate a small seven-day change in schedule. Right?

Right! In fact, the family adjusted rather well. It was me that had the problem. What all of us reunion planners forgot was that the reason the family gathering has been such a howling success over the past several years is our reunion (more aptly described as a bunch of people who like to eat a lot) coincides with our church's annual chicken barbecue. Consequently, bride-woman's menu planning and food preparation have always been held to a minimum. She made some iced tea, carved up a couple of watermelons, chilled some soft drinks, and kept everyone happy until it was time to feed the troops.

Then all we had to do was get a chow line organized and head for the First Church of Big Miracles. The talented ladies at the church did the rest. The family ate high on the hen. We loaded up on baked beans, slaw, homemade pies, ice cream, and went away (if not totally happy, at least totally full). Bottom line ... successful reunion.

The Curmudgeon Rides Again

This year, however, this annual circus we call our reunion occurs the week after the chicken-chapel fest. Leaving us with the somewhat perplexing problem of how much food to prepare for the revelers.

Question: How many hamburgers do you prepare for some 60 dedicated eaters? Eaters range in age from 86 years old to 6 months. Easy, you say. According to Moonbeam's party book, you should figure on 1 and ½ burgers per person. But wait, there is an onion in the woodpile. When you read something like that you wonder if they took into account the handful of teenage boys in attendance. A couple of these youngsters could inhale a whole cow without half trying.

After you get beyond the mystery of the burgers, you have a few other mealtime questions to consider. What are you going to serve in addition to the sandwiches? When my bride asked me what I thought would go with hamburgers, I suggested sleeping pills. That way, after chowing down, everyone would take naps and when they woke up the reunion would be over. How's that for quick thinking?

For me, a reunion is one of those lose-lose situations everyone talks about. If they don't take naps, they will all gather around the piano and sing all day.

At any rate, after settling on the issue of food, there is always the matter of entertainment. Last year we had a magician. He asked me what kinds of legerdemain I wanted him to perform. I asked him if he could make the whole reunion disappear. He said he couldn't do that, so I asked him if he could make Moonbeam's Uncle Harold disappear. He said he couldn't do that either. I don't think he was much of a magician. In any case, I'm not inviting him back until he can do a few of the tricks I'm interested in.

The year before the magician, Moonbeam had Harley Trump, the impressionist, provide the entertainment. When I asked the family what they thought, they said they weren't impressed. I guess they thought his impression of a sick cat, two turtles courting, and especially the one of ice melting left a little to be desired.

All that aside, we're putting the final touches on food and entertainment for this year's reunion. And even though it pains me to say it, I think we're ready. We have lots of really fun type activities planned. Our neighbor is scheduled to empty his septic tank at 11:00. At noon, Uncle Harlan is bringing his goat, Esmerelda, over to eat grass. Then we're all going into town to watch our nephew, Gerald, get a haircut.

Sound exciting?

I know what you are thinking ... but hear me out. There is a method to my madness. With activities like the ones we have planned this year, I can almost guarantee Moonbeam will not ask for my help next year.

"Meetings are indispensable if you don't want to accomplish anything or kill a little time." John Kenneth Galbraith
Ambassador's Journal 1969

How do you feel about birthday parties?

More specifically, how do you feel about having a birthday and someone throwing a party to help you celebrate?

If you're young, like my grandson's age, you can't wait to be grown up. If you're my age, you probably wish they weren't mounting up so rapidly.

If it wasn't that birthdays are some sort of indication that we are still treading water amidst the flotsam in the stream of life, I'd just as soon forget them.

Think about this. When you are young, every birthday is a big deal. There are all kinds of milestones and benchmarks to be achieved by such and such a birthday. By the time you're one year old you are walking. When your second birthday rolls around you're out of diapers. By your third birthday, you are dazzling your grandparents with your extensive vocabulary of twenty to thirty words. At six you start school and you follow up with a bunch of important birthdays that allow you to date, drive a car, register for the draft, achieve voting age, etc. Then, all of a sudden, you discover there isn't a whole lot to be achieved by getting older. Suddenly, you start worrying about your weight, your blood pressure, and a whole lot of other indicators that you are starting to pile up birthdays.

What brings all this on?

A birthday! I got older last week. Officially, I am one whole year older. The calendar says it's just one year, but I feel like it has been a great deal longer than that. When you're my age and another birthday rolls around, it is not cause for a *&% birthday party. If anything, it's a sigh of relief I should be uttering. Against all odds, we have survived another year.

Having said all of that, let's get to the heart of the matter. I don't like parties. Most of all, I don't like birthday parties. Birthday parties are sorta like bragging that a person gets to pay life insurance premiums for another year.

If you're smart, you don't brag about having survived for another year. You keep quiet and hope you can sneak up on another twelve months. If you're lumbago permits and you think you'll be able to get back up again, you might even try kneeling down and saying a prayer of thanks.

Of all the types of birthday parties I don't like, the ones I don't like the most are the ones where you go out to dinner with

My Favorite Holiday Hasn't Been Invented Yet

your family and someone tips off the waiter or waitress that you are having a birthday. If that happens, at the end of the meal, four or five overly exuberant, off-key grinning server types gather around your table and sing some idiotic, cutesy birthday song that usually ends up with a cha cha cha.

At Joe's Crab Shack in Fort Wayne the birthday boy or girl suffers total humiliation. The Crab people insist that the individual don a cowboy hat and pretend a broom is your horse. Then you run around the room making, not a horse, but an ass of yourself.

Been there?

Ain't it awful?

Hey, it can and often does get worse. If you're my age, every stiff in the room sits there grinning, watching you try to gum your birthday Jell-O into a substance you can swallow. Is the reason they are smiling because they are happy for you? No way, Jose. They are all extremely glad it was you who endured the embarrassment instead of them.

While I prefer to acknowledge the fact that I survived another year on good, old *terra firma* in the quietest way possible, my bride-woman wants the entire world to share the joyous anniversary of her birth with her. If Moonbeam had her way, she would prefer banners across the driveway, an announcement in the *Herald-Republican*, a rather large cake with Paul Newman poking out of it and three or four hundred of her closest friends gathered around the campfire singing songs of cheery jocundity.

If the alternative to another birthday wasn't a plot at Circle Hill Cemetery, I'd say what's the big deal? For the most part, age *ain't* kind. My poker-playing buddies can't read their cards anymore ... and the rest of my pals can't lift their glasses to celebrate because of their hernias. The drink of choice is no longer choice ... it is carrot juice or V8 (doctor's orders). Even worse, most of us are threatened with terminal baldness.

Celebrate? I don't think so. I can't hear the numbers at bingo. I can't remember my hole card in five card stud. I can't even remember what I think when someone asks for my opinion. When I turn on the television to watch the Cubs play, I fall asleep. I guess I should mention though that this is one of the few advantages to being an old Cub fan. You can take lots of naps during the course of the game and generally you don't miss much.

Birthdays? My friends have lost so many teeth they have cake soup on their birthday. I had so many candles on my birthday cake this year, Moonbeam stood by with a garden hose in case the fire got out of hand. The smoke alarms went off.

The Orland Fire Department sent a representative over to the house to inform us there is an ordinance against uncontrolled burning.

By the time I blew the candles out, the ceiling was singed. Happy birthday? Yeah, right.

My favorite toast: "Absinthe makes the tart grow fonder." attributed to Hugh Drummond, 1943

How are you doing with your New Year's resolutions? I'm sure this won't surprise you when I tell you most of my friends are already treating their resolutions this year the same way they have in the past. In other words, they have already broken them.

This is a delicate issue, but I'll get into it anyway. Now if you just happen to be one of those folks who has fallen off the resolution wagon in a matter of hours after the new year arrived (and I'm not saying you are), don't feel like one of those weak-kneed souls short on steadfastness that our pastors like to refer to

My Favorite Holiday Hasn't Been Invented Yet

(even though you may be one).

Granted, you may actually be one of those self-indulging twits just like yours truly, but if you are ever going to pull off this New Year resolution gig, you can't act like one.

Let's discuss the built-in pitfalls in this annual cave-in to feeble frailties. First of all, statistics show that by noon on New Year's Day, fully half of the people that made resolutions have broken half of their resolutions. What this means is some folks go to a New Year's party, get home about six o'clock in the morning, go to bed, sleep a couple of hours, get up and promptly break one or more of their resolutions. Sound familiar?

What resolution is most frequently broken on the first day, you ask? Answer? Smoking. What is second? Dieting.

These were the two resolutions I made every year for a number of years. I was pretty confident I could get up on New Year's Day and make it through breakfast without breaking my resolution on dieting. Sure it was tough (but hey, I'm a tough guy), still, I usually made it. Occasionally I would make it all the way to noon without smoking my pipe.

Then, the resolution maker's best friend took over. It's called *rationalization*. Hey, I had already given up food. Did they expect me to give up my pipe as well? (I'm not sure who "they" were ... but darn 'em anyway.) At any rate, the rationalization process goes something like this: Giving up smoking and going on a diet all in one day is too much to expect of anyone. Furthermore, I'm sure no one (not even my staunchest critics) expected me to solve all my problems at once.

Bottom line? By that evening, intellectualizing and self vindication allowed me to watch the Rose Bowl with a monster bowl of munchies and a periodic reflective pipe.

Finally, I took the advice of a friend who taught me how to make resolutions I could live with. "Learn to make resolutions that aren't so difficult to keep," he suggested. "After you learn to

The Curmudgeon Rides Again

keep simple resolutions, you'll feel much better about the whole process of making resolutions. Why? Because you will have developed confidence ... confidence that you are going to be able to keep the resolutions you make."

It sounded like the kind of advice I could live with. So I made two resolutions I was reasonably certain I could keep. First, I promised my wife I would not try to jog around the lake every day. Second, I resolved not to gorge myself on carrots and broccoli.

How did I do? I did great. I developed the concept of compensators. When I felt the urge to jog around the lake, I forced myself to take a nap. When I felt like eating carrots and broccoli, I ate a Snickers bar instead.

After six months had passed, I hadn't faltered (not even once) on either resolution. Remarkable self control? Well, that's what I call it. Fact is, I was feeling so good about myself at that point that I made two more resolutions. One, to give up crocodile wrestling for once and all. Two, I promised myself I would not miss any of my Tuesday night poker club meetings. Once again, it was not easy, but I succeeded.

Assessment? I had evolved from the type of individual who was unable to sustain a resolution through day one of the new year to one who had conquered and kept four difficult resolutions in one year.

I don't want to brag, but after that I began piling up the "kept resolutions" and I rapidly became a paragon of resolution-keeping discipline. I soon gave up the compulsive and disgusting habit of cleaning my studio once a month (once a year works fine). I sacrificed taking out the garbage and turned the chore over to my wife so that she could benefit from the exercise. I quit calling the cat names (she couldn't understand me anyway), and I learned to talk about some of Moonbeam's relatives without giggling. (I still giggle about some of them, but the ones I giggle

My Favorite Holiday Hasn't Been Invented Yet

about weren't included in that resolution.)

This year I went way out on the limb with three church-related resolutions. One, I'm going to quit humming Beatles tunes to myself during Pastor Good's sermons. I have enough confidence in myself now that I really believe I can stay awake during the entire sermon. Two, I promise to quit running across the sanctuary to the coffee/donut bar after the service. Besides, I now know I can get there first with just a fast walk. Three, I will quit putting counter checks written with disappearing ink in the collection basket. I don't think the ushers thought it was as funny as I did.

> "My advice is not to take life too seriously. No matter what you do, you will not get out of it alive."
> Elbert Hubbard

Remember that old expression, "A day late and a dollar short?"

Whoever said that was talking about me. Yesterday was National Clean Up Your Office Day and I forgot all about it until I looked at my daily planning calendar last night as I was going to bed.

Surprised? If you are I'll let you in on a secret. I am a procrastinator. If I can find a way to put something off, I'll do it. Knowing this I have finally devised a way to get myself involved in getting the things done that must be done. I tell myself that the entire world is doing that particular chore on that particular day and I don't want to look bad by not contributing. Hence: NCUYOD or National Clean Up Your Office Day.

Second admission: it is Saturday afternoon, it is raining, and I am as reluctant to get started today as I would have been yesterday if I had known that I was supposed to do it then. However, I am staring at the cluttered bulletin board over my computer (all writers have cluttered bulletin boards over their computers), and I do recognize this clean up chore is long overdue.

The bulletin board is important. It is where I keep everything that is crucial to my writing. For example, I have a calendar. The fact that it is a 1988 calendar is neither here nor there. But it is testimony to the fact that my beloved bulletin board isn't subjected to frequent and unnecessary purges.

It is also testimony to the fact that I live in fear that some yo-yo from the Internal Revenue Service is going to call any day now, checking on some detail of my return that year. Why 1988? I'm intuitive about these things. At any rate, I better leave that calendar right where it is.

Next to the calendar is a picture of our foursome at the annual company golf tournament back in 1985. I don't work for that company anymore. I keep the picture because we had a lot of fun that day. I still laugh when I think about my boss driving our golf cart into the pond on the fourth hole. Of course, I don't look back too fondly on the fact that we all had to chip in two hundred and fifty dollars to make things right with the guy in the pro shop.

Two things about that incident still amaze me. First, I never realized a water hazard could be that deep. Second, the course ranger looked pretty healthy to me. I had no idea he would darn near drown trying to retrieve the cart. At any rate, I better leave that picture right where it is. It's a reminder not to try to play golf there again.

Next to that picture is a valentine from Moonbeam. She

My Favorite Holiday Hasn't Been Invented Yet

sent it to me in 1981. I wonder where her more recent valentines are? The cartoon picture of the guy on the front of the card looks a lot like her Uncle Harold. Harold is always good for a few laughs. He's the one who lost his bathing suit while he was water skiing here at the lake a couple of summers ago. Actually, no one even noticed except his wife. She didn't think much about it. She said with Harold there wasn't all that much to see.

I also have a coaster pinned on the bulletin board. It came from Sloppy Joe's down in Key West. It's made of a blotter kind of material that is supposed to soak up spilled beer. I got that coaster the day I went to pay homage to Ernest Hemingway. I keep it there just in case someone throws a beer at me and it hits the bulletin board.

Down in the right hand corner I have a copy of the royalty check from my first book. I never knew anyone issued checks for less than a dollar.

There are a lot of pictures on my bulletin board. There is one of my mother (the Democrat) and her brothers Arlo and Olin. They were both Republicans and from the expressions on their faces, it looks like they weren't real excited about having their picture taken with a registered Democrat. I guess I better leave that right where it is as well.

Let's see. Hey, look at this. Here is something I forgot was even up there ... a copy of my New Year's resolutions for 1994. I wonder what's on that list? Yup. Well, I'll be darned. Can you imagine that? Hmmm. Really? Think I better leave that right where it is as well. Looks to me like it's the same list of resolutions I make every year. If I leave it where it is I won't have to make out a new list this coming New Year.

Almost hidden by my list of resolutions is another interesting item ... my expired driver's license. I don't think I look as old as that picture on my license makes me look. As I recall I put that up there two years ago to remind me to get a new driver's

The Curmudgeon Rides Again

license. Better leave it there. I'm forgetful and I'll forget to get it renewed if I take it down.

Ah ha! What's this? Holy smoke, it's an article on the sinking of the *Edmund Fitzgerald*. That happened in November of 1975? Gosh, how time flies. I've always intended to write something about that. Better leave it right where it is or I'll forget about it.

Back to the pictures. Here is one of Frankenstein getting a shave in a barbershop. (Actually it isn't really Frankenstein; just an actor dressed up like him.) I put that picture on my bulletin board to remind me that I have to broaden my horizons and think more creatively. Giving Frankenstein a shave is something I never would have thought of. Would you?

Here's a gem. It's a picture of Marilyn Monroe. She doesn't have any clothes on. Wonder why I saved that?

What's this? I'll be darned. It's a note from my daughter. It says, "Mom called. The car stalled on the way home from work and she wants you to pick her up." Son-of-a-gun, wonder when that happened?

I suppose I better have a talk with my daughter. She should be told that anything resembling an emergency should never be put on my bulletin board. Better yet, I'll make a note to myself to tell her that. But what will I do with it until I see her?

I know ... I'll put it right here on the bulletin board.

"How can you whistle while you work if you are a librarian?"
Groucho Marx

Mother's Day, 1993.

Mother's Day ... the day when we search out some syr-

My Favorite Holiday Hasn't Been Invented Yet

upy, but truly heartfelt, card that tries to convey how everyone (well, almost *everyone*) feels about their mothers.

My own mother was a sucker for Mother's Day. She enjoyed every minute of every Mother's Day she ever celebrated. The fact that I was her only son and that she lived long enough to see how I turned out, never seemed to deter her from the fact that she was still proud of being a mother.

I called my mother Mom and I am quick to point out she was not your typical mother ... at least not the way we used to think of mothers in bygone days. I realize now that Mom was caught in a time warp between the "then" and the "now." She was liberated (for her time), but she wore dresses, had her hair done and was pretty. She was, and the feminists out there will probably cringe when they hear me say it, *a real lady.*

But that's where the typical *Mom* role stopped.

Her idea of a Mother's Day card was one of those oversized greeting cards with a pink and white, heart-shaped satin pillow in the center with a message that said something incredibly innovative like "Happy Mother's Day."

On the other hand, her idea of the perfect gift would have been two airline tickets and a hotel room at the Democratic National Convention.

The biggest hit I ever made with a Mother's Day gift was the time I gave her an 8 x 10-inch picture of John and Jackie Kennedy. Mom put it in the fanciest gold frame she could find at Woolworth's and sat it on top of her TV set. Every time I sat down to watch a Cubs game on television, I had to look at it. Mom knew this. She also knew how I had voted in the previous election. She enjoyed every one of my tortured moments.

Mom never understood that boys like to be hugged ... but only in private. Never in front of a bunch of other guys. In my junior year in high school, our school played South Side. In the second quarter, some guy wearing Archer green knocked me silly and I was escorted (actually I was carried, but what macho teenage boy wants to admit he was "carried") to the sidelines. The next thing I remember, my mother was leaning over me, surrounded by team members and coaching staff, kissing my broken nose and telling me she would "make it all better."

I've got news for you, that kind of talk in front of 60 muscle bound, primarily testosterone motivated, teenage males changed their perspective of my budding manhood. You should have heard what they called me in the locker room.

My mother was never one to let the follies of my youth escape unnoticed. She walked out of the house one night while a bunch of my buddies and I were playing basketball and announced that she had a gift for me. She then proceeded to hand me a new Gillette razor, complete with a package of razor blades. Everything would have been cool and my buddies would have been impressed if she hadn't added, "It's time you had your own razor. Now you can quit using mine."

The chorus of giggles and guffaws was instantaneous. The next thing I heard was, "You mean you've been using your mom's razor? The same one she uses to shave her legs?"

Total teenage humiliation.

On another occasion, Mom knew I was having difficulty getting a date for the school prom. (Actually, I had trouble getting a date for every social function our school had ... but that's another story.) The first girl I asked smugly told me she was going with the class president. Girl number two declined because her favorite TV program was on that night. The third girl declined because she said she couldn't dance. The fourth girl declined because she said I couldn't dance. Girl five couldn't go because the prom conflicted with her acne treatment appointment.

Mom knew all this and that's when she stepped in. She got me a date with one telephone call. When I asked her how she did it, she informed me that she knew Twyla Fernwald was enter-

My Favorite Holiday Hasn't Been Invented Yet

ing the convent in a matter of weeks and Mom figured she would probably like to go to at least one dance before she joined the order.

Mom never took into consideration that Twyla was a good six inches taller than me and that dancing was going to be a contortionistic affair for both of us. On the bright side, we did get the most votes for funkiest couple at the dance.

How many guys do you know who went to the most important dance of their high school years with a wantabe nun? In case I didn't mention it, Twyla was already becoming a nun. Other girls wore formals to the prom. Twyla wore a habit. She insisted I introduce her to my friends as Sister Mary Twyla.

What kind of dance step do you do with someone who is humming "Ave Maria?"

When the rest of the kids started necking after the prom, Twyla expected me to kneel down with her and pray. I did. I prayed the night would end.

I still remember when Mom got me my first puppy. She was the one who named the puppy, Mr. Poopie. She insisted I get my picture taken with Mr. Poopie. I was sixteen.

Oh well, like I say, I still remember that first razor and the day when I finally had to put a blade in the darn thing.

I still remember that picture of John and Jackie Kennedy.

I still remember ...

By the way, Mom, how's the weather up there?

> "My wife is a good driver. After she parallel parks she only has a short walk to the sidewalk."
> Murray Anderson

There we were. Just the two of us. Smiling faces. Gifts exchanged. Presents unwrapped. Full of and fulfilled by the gift of giving spirit of a splendid and joyous Yuletide.

Time to relax?

I don't think so.

Time to kick back, savor, enjoy ... right?

Guess again. In other words, *"No way."* That's not the way it works around our house.

"Now," Moonbeam, my longtime spouse and the mother of all organizers announces, " ... let's talk about our New Year's resolutions."

"Wait a minute," I said, treading water, "I'm still trying to get started on two of this year's resolutions: I've still got 30 pounds to lose this week and I want to write a book on how to avoid becoming a procrastinator before next Sunday."

"Look," Moonbeam says, "I know New Year's resolutions are hard to keep. I was only able to read 48 of the 50 'self help' books I intended to read this year. I'm only walking six miles a day instead of seven. I only floss my teeth five times a day instead of the ..."

"All right," I mutter (I know when I'm spiraling down to certain defeat), " ... what kind of resolutions?" For those of you who don't recognize it, the handwriting is on the wall ... this is clearly going to be one of those conversations I dread. (Incidentally, not writing on the wall was one of my resolutions back in 1996.)

"I thought it would be a good idea," she smiled, " ... if we

My Favorite Holiday Hasn't Been Invented Yet

made New Year's resolutions for each other. You make five for me that will help me become a better person and I will make five for you with the same objective."

"Wait a minute," I said, " ... let me get this straight. You want me to make five resolutions for you that will, if you keep them for a whole year, make you a better person. Gee, I don't think I can do that. I mean, don't you first have to have five little faults that need correcting?" (Am I good at this marriage game or am I good at this marriage game?) I know what's at stake here; this is clearly no time for brain fade. Finally though, just in case she missed the subtlety in my approach, I say, "I'd have to think pretty hard to come up with five resolutions for you. You don't have that many faults."

Moonbeam ignores my slavish response. "By the same token, I would have to come up with five resolutions for you," my bride smiled.

"Guess you'd have to think about that a long time too," I said.

"Not really," she told me. "Here they are in fact. I typed the list, had copies made so you'll always be aware of what you have to work on this year."

"I thought this was a spur of the moment idea."

"Oh, it was," she smiled, "I'll even help you get started on resolution number one: cleaning up your studio."

Before you read further, two things need further explanation in this little epistle. First of all, it is very difficult to drag your feet on a project when someone offers to help you get started. But I was doing it. When Moonbeam suggested it, at that particular moment, I just wasn't in the mood to start tidying up my studio. (The truth of the matter is I haven't been in the mood to tidy up my studio for the last twenty years.)

Secondly, who knows when the mood will (if ever) strike me? I prefer to think of it as creative clutter, clutter is my kingdom and I am the king. (I have these little flights of fancy every now and then.)

Moonbeam's second resolution suggestion has to do with a commitment on my part to keep Freight Train (our dog) out of certain parts of the house. My bride thinks that just because Freight Train stands roughly thirty-six inches high at the shoulder, weighs about eighty pounds and eats cows, her run of the house should be restricted.

"Which parts of the house don't you want her in?" I ask.

"The living room, the family room, any of the bedrooms, any of the bathrooms, guest rooms, kitchen, dining room ... actually no where in the house except your studio."

"But I thought you wanted me to clean up my studio," I said.

"I'm certain you'll be able to work it out," bride-woman smiles, " ... besides, I think you're getting the drift ... an animal that size doesn't belong in the house."

It hasn't even started yet and I'm beginning to get the feeling the new year isn't going to be my favorite year. I was almost afraid to ask, "What's resolution number three?"

"Last year you promised to work on not snoring during the Sunday sermon," she reminded me. "Maybe we ought to revisit that one. You closed your eyes, tilted your head to one side, and made funny little noises all through the sermon last week."

"Wait a minute," I protested, " ... you're not saying I can't sleep, you're just saying I can't snore."

"I would never ask the impossible," Moonbeam assured me.

"If that's the case," I said, " ... then let's forget that first resolution. You know, the one about me finally cleaning my studio."

"Why is that?" Moonbeam wanted to know.

"Because keeping resolution number three isn't near as impossible as keeping resolution number one."

It's A Guy Thing

"Actually, there is a vast difference between the brute savage and civilized man. However, that difference is never apparent to their wives until after breakfast."
> Helen Rowland
> *A Guide to Men*

Every time my wife and I pass a man leaning on a shovel or she sees one of my friends with a death grip on the TV remote, she asks me why? I tell her the simple and irrefutable truth: It's a guy thing.

When a car quits, the first thing a man does is get out of the car, open the hood, and stand there scratching his head. That's a guy thing, too.

When a man gets lost, drives around in circles, and refuses to ask directions as his wife suggests, that's a guy thing as well.

By now women should know, men are supposed to lean on shovels. That's the way their fathers taught them. Right?

By now you women should know that all men know how to act like they know how to fix what's wrong with cars. Right?

By now all women should know that all men are would-be explorers. They are never lost. Right?

Spitting, belching, scratching ... those are all guy things. And if you just happen to be one of those people who know a woman that exhibits similar behavior; trust me, she learned that behavior from some guy.

I, for one, have always been intrigued by the stream of complaints women have regarding their male counterparts. The way I see it, women complaining about men is a little like complaining about a bad hair day. There isn't a whole lot you can do about it except cut it off.

I have advice for women who have nothing but complaints about men. It's simple. If you don't want one hanging around the house, quit feeding it. Sooner or later it will go away.

How did we get to where we are today? Not surprisingly, I have a theory about men (as I do most things), their behavior, and how they became what they have become.

According to the Bible, God was sitting around one day, feeling a bit out of sorts, started fooling around and invented a man. This, in scientific journals, is referred to as Man One.

The important thing to note is he made Man One before he made anything else (including Woman One). Not having a whole lot of practice at this man making thing, Man One had a few chinks in his design. Not only was he an ugly dude (he looked a lot like an ape), he was impatient. He complained and grumbled that he had nothing to do and nowhere to go.

So God invented the universe.

Man One continued to complain, bewail, and lament.

Hearing that, God invented beer and baseball.

Still not satisfied with his lot in life, Man One moaned and groaned, "Who am I going to talk to?" Whereupon, God in-

It's A Guy Thing

vented dogs (his crowning achievement there was the Golden Retriever).

Soon, Man One was caviling and carping about living conditions again and God became exasperated.

"I'll fixth your wagon," God said.

(Note: I'm not exactly certain how God really talks. By that I mean, whether he says things like "loveth" and uses the word "thee" and things like that. However, that's the way they talk in the Bible according to the guys like Moses who actually had conversations with the Big Guy. Therefore one assumes they know how he talked.)

"What's a wagon?" Man One sayth (sounds more like an actual conversation from the Old Testament, doesn't it?).

"As soon as I inventith you one, I'll fixth yours," God said. Whereupon God quickly built a wagon, fixed it, gave it to Man One, and then he invented Woman One. As he gave her a final shape, he whispered in her ear. "That son-of-a-gunneth has done nothing buy bellyacheth since I madeth him. I want to teach him a lesson. Go forth and make him sorry he was such a whiner. Make him realize how good he actually had it."

Well, as Paul Harvey so often says, "Now you know the rest of the story." Man spits, woman complains. Man scratches, woman tells him to quit. Man belches, and woman is disgusted. About the only thing they haven't mastered is leaning on a shovel and opening the hood of a car so they can scratch their heads.

The Curmudgeon Rides Again

> "Love is a way with meaning for a woman. Sex is meaning enough for a man."
> Charles Bukowski
> *Notes of a Dirty Old Man*

Have you ever had one of those days when it just didn't make a whole lot of sense to get up?

Last Sunday was one of those days for me. If I had known what kind of day it was going to be, I probably would have just stayed in bed and pretended I was sick.

Sundays around our house are somewhat ritualistic. First, there is church. Then, there is whatever we are going to do after church. Finally, there is the rest of the day and how that goes pretty much depends on the weather.

The Sunday I am reflecting back on began, as always, with making certain Freight Train (she plays the role of the dog in our domicile) gets out before anything nasty happens. Normally this is not a difficult chore but on the Sunday in question it was raining. Pouring would be a better word.

Having eliminated any possibility of returning to the sack (I was now soaking wet.), I opted for a shower to get me kick started. In the shower I discovered there was no soap. So, soaking wet (this time from the shower), I found it necessary to get out of the shower, go to Moonbeam's supply closet, fetch (I like the word *fetch*.) new soap and return.

After a vigorous shower, I was confronted with the fact I had forgotten a towel. Off to the linen closet. Luckily the rest of my "get up" ritual came off without a hitch.

Did I mention that when I went into my studio, I discovered one of my goldfish had jumped out of his watery abode and was laying there, eyes open even in death, trying to figure out what happened? Like I always say, death is a harsh lesson. I'll bet Sam (the goldfish) knows that now. Of course, the information isn't going to do him much good.

At church that Sunday we had a guest minister. Guest ministers are a change of pace. They preach about different things. Our regular minister has been preaching on the same subject for nearly a year now. I think he lost the other parts of his Bible.

Halfway through the service my grandson had to go to the restroom. Have you ever noticed that kids can sit through an entire two and a half hour movie without having to go to the bathroom? But the minute they get in church something happens to their plumbing.

After the worship service, we have coffee and donuts in the fellowship area. I don't know why they call it the fellowship area. There are more women there than men. Maybe it should be called the womanship area. In the fellowship area you are supposed to put a dollar in the basket before you take your coffee and donut. I didn't have anything but a twenty dollar bill. I put in the twenty and started to make change. Three women were watching me. I think they thought I was taking money out of the donut fund.

After church we often go to Pokagon for the brunch. If you don't have a season pass, you have to pay a small fee at the gate. When I started to hand the girl the money, I dropped it. It rolled under the car. I had to get out of the car, get down on my hands and knees, and look for my money. In the meantime, the cars lined up behind our car started honking their horns. I guess they must have been hungry. That seems to happen when it's raining.

Things didn't go much better at brunch. I was last in the omelet line. I spilled my coffee on my Sunday pants. When I

The Curmudgeon Rides Again

went to pay for breakfast, I discovered that I had left my wallet in the car. I had taken it out of my pocket when I had to pay my gate fee. So, leaving Moonbeam as collateral at the cashier's station, I ran down the hill to the garage, retrieved my wallet, got soaking wet, and returned to pay my bill. That's when the cashier, seeing me drip all over her counter asked, "Is it still raining?"

By the time we returned to our sanctuary of sanity, I had stopped to purchase gas, gotten wet again, and convinced my grandson we didn't have time for him to fill out all the forms required to win a year's supply of bubble gum.

When Moonbeam saw me marching up the stairs, disrobing as I went, she wanted to know what was happening. "I'm going back to bed," I said, " ... then I'm starting the day over."

> **"The whole motivation for any man is the learning that comes from the period in his life when he shouted, 'Look at me, Ma.'"**
> **Lenny Bruce**

We were having dinner the other night with some friends when one of the women at the table sallied forth with one of those feminist comments that turns a quiet dinner into a battle zone.

"Men are absolutely helpless without women," she said, " ... but the way I see it, women can get along quite well without men."

Bad? You bet. But to make matters worse, when I looked across the table at my long time spouse, she was smiling and nodding her head in agreement.

"For example," the woman went on, " ... when my brother got a divorce, he fell apart. He couldn't take care of himself. He couldn't get organized. He couldn't even think straight."

(Side comment: It doesn't take a divorce to put lots of guys I know in that condition. A couple of beers and a bowl of chili will usually do it too.)

"Wait a minute," I said, coming up for air. "I suppose you're going to tell me that a woman doesn't have problems after a divorce?"

"Oh, she might grieve a little," the woman admitted, " ... but for the most part she goes on with her life pretty much as though nothing has happened. After all, what has she lost?"

Before I could launch a counterattack, mouth-woman was firing a second volley.

"Women have more friends; they talk to their girlfriends on the phone. They chat about girl things. They are just not as lonely because they can always fall back on universal sisterhood of women for support. Men, on the other hand, don't have as many friends and since all they ever talk about are shallow things like sports, they don't know how to talk about real life things like loneliness and feelings."

"Lots of guys can talk about that kind of stuff," I protested. "I know a single guy, Bert Plimpton. When Bert lost his hunting dog, Mabel, he cried one night when we went out for a beer. If that isn't talking about loneliness, what is?"

"See," she said, " ... that's exactly what I mean. Men are just plain uncomfortable talking about their feelings and their problems. Don't you realize your friend's real loneliness stems from something far deeper than losing his hunting dog? He just refuses to face it."

"Well, you could be right about that in Bert's case," I admitted. "Someone did take his pickup truck. His favorite shot gun was in it, but they left the truck and the gun down at the gas station the next night."

"A hunting dog, a pickup truck, and a shot gun," she

snarled. "Isn't that a sad commentary on a man's life? No plans, no social commitments, no personal growth, absolutely no culture."

"What do you mean?" I stammered. I was getting a bit defensive. "Bert has social commitments and culture. His social calendar is so full he doesn't have time for those other things you keep talking about. Why, every Friday night he goes down to the Cesspool Bar and Grill and drinks beer with his buddies. On Saturday night he plays poker and every fourth Sunday he goes over to his parents' house so his mother can do his laundry."

"See," adversary woman thundered, " ... men don't even know how to clean up after themselves."

When she said that she started to get my hackles up. "What do you mean, 'clean up after ourselves?' You make it sound like we're not even potty trained."

"Does your friend, Bert, wash his dishes on a regular basis?" she pressed.

"Every two weeks or whenever the sink gets full," I countered.

"That's what I mean. A woman is taught from childhood to be orderly, self-sufficient, and self-reliant. Therefore she can do everything for herself. Men, on the other hand, are taught to be competitive and masculine. Tell me," she said, " ... what niceties of life do you think your friend has?"

Another confession is appropriate here. Being a writer, I tend to think somewhat better when I write than when I talk. I started making a list. "Let me tell you about Bert's niceties," I told her. "My friend, Bert, has a pickup truck, bought a puppy to replace Mabel, plays poker a couple of times a week, watches all the baseball and football games he wants to watch on television, never has to give up the remote control on his television, has three kinds of beer in his cooler, and eats pizza three nights a week."

"Isn't that pathetic," the woman said.

"Yup. Sure is," I said. I don't think she saw me winking at the other guys around the table when I said it though.

"To be a good politician, you've got to ignore the facts."
Henry Brooks Adams
The Scoundrels Guide to Politics

Do you ever read the personals? That's the page you find in some newspapers where folks advertise that they are available and looking. It's sort of a modern day spin on what we guys used to do when we would to go a dance and stand on the sidelines watching the girls. The big difference between then and now is that the girls are out there looking too.

Nowadays if you want to meet someone of the opposite sex, you don't get all duded up, slick back your hair, and hang out in the stag line. You simply run an ad in the personals. Then all you have to do is sit by the phone and hope you've generated some interest. It's sorta like fishing with fake worms. Throw out your best line and hope someone takes the bait.

Sound like a nifty approach?

Perhaps. But there is a small hurdle to overcome first. To be any good at this game, you have to understand the lingo and the abbreviations these folks use to describe themselves, their interests, and the kind of person they are looking for.

Take for example the following: *"Sensitive, music loving, romantic, full figured, SWF, 45, 5'6", enjoys dancing, movies, candlelight dinners, hiking, rock music, and horses. Seeking neat, honest, reliable, humorous, free-spirited SWM, NS, who enjoys travel."*

So exactly what is she saying?

First of all, be aware, this lady is either less than honest or is confused. She claims to be a music lover then proceeds to confess she likes rock music. This is what is known as a blatant contradiction.

Next, notice that she describes herself as *"full figured."* A little further into her brief resume, she mentions the fact that she likes *"candlelight dinners."* Once again this is where it is important to understand the lingo. With this *SWF* (single white female), *candlelight dinners* and *full-figured* equate to liking to eat. Maybe even, liking to eat a whole lot. But, and this is definitely a point in her favor, she is telling you up front that she doesn't expect to be hauled off to Fast Food Freddy or Chicken Charlie kinds of places. She digs the expensive places: flowers on the table, candles and tablecloths. She will probably even expect you to know how to eat with your fork instead of your fingers.

All of this, my female-companion-seeking friend, computes to meaning she is looking for someone with enough golden grinkles in his bank account to take her to the finer places when chow time rolls around.

Are you starting to see how this game is played?

Now let's look at the rest of the advertisement. She mentions *"horses."* She doesn't say anything about *"riding horses."* Reduced to its obvious meaning, in all likelihood this means she likes to go to the racetrack and bet on the ponies. How have I deduced that? You have to read between the lines. Think about it. Cozy candlelight dinners and trail riding are activities at the opposite end of the entertainment spectrum. This *SWF* sure doesn't sound like a can-of-beans-in-the-frying-pan-around-the-old-campfire-lady to me.

But let's not stop here. Let's learn all we can from this

example. Taking into account all that has been mentioned above, the lady is either unrealistic, unreasonable or both. She says she wants to meet a man who is *"honest, neat, reliable, and free spirited."*

Get real. Does such a man exist?

Show me a man with all of those sterling attributes and both political parties would be trying to pressure him into running for president. Besides, if such a man existed, some clever woman would have him nuptualized by now.

Now let's try one for the girls. Try this one. *"Attractive, loyal, very affectionate, SWM, 25, 6'2", athletic, enjoys working out, music, movies, and romantic evenings. Seeking attractive SWF for possible LTR.* (Gee, this guy must look and think just like me ... if I was looking that is.)

First of all, all you gals out there, ask yourself, what kind of guy calls himself *"attractive?"* Attractive is a sissy word. Good looking guys might refer to themselves as "personable," "studly," or "not hard to look at" ... but never *"attractive."* If any of you gals out there decide to follow up on this cat, find out what kind of underwear he wears. If it's pink, forget him.

Chances are, if he is legitimate, he will spend more time looking into the mirror to admire himself than he will your eyes. And here's another thing, notice how this guy claimed to be an athlete. If that's the case, his idea of a "workout" may be chasing you around your living room so he can get his exercise.

Girls, always (underline the word "always") be careful when you see a personal ad with some guy heading his resume Dr. Love or Meet Mr. Wonderful. Truth in advertising doesn't apply to personals.

Let me show you how misleading this can all be.

"Affectionate, middle aged, SF, never married, home-loving, has own home, enjoys walks, gentle companion, and fire-

The Curmudgeon Rides Again

places."

Interested? If so, I can fix you up with our dog Freight Train.

"Is it hot in the coal mines? Are the hours long? Is 15 bucks an hour not enough? Then try something different. Walk away from your old job, hock your soul to buy a word processor, and write another, 'Hunt For Red October.' Trust me, buying the word processor will be the easy part."
James V. Smith Jr., Author

Ever have one of those days when you just don't feel like doing anything?

I'm talking about the kind of day when you are actually proud of your status as a couch potato.

... Or the kind of day when you figure out a way to justify procrastinating on just about everything.

... Or the kind of day when you go to the refrigerator, open the door, and nothing looks good.

... Or you surf the channels on your TV set and nothing looks interesting.

Had one of those have you?

Well, last week I had one of those days. I was tired of my CD's, bored with reading, didn't feel like being sociable, and I sure didn't feel like helping Moonbeam put away the Christmas paraphernalia.

"I feel like the wart on a hog's nose," I informed my bride. "I'm in a blue funk. What can I do to get out of this mood?"

"Write down your thoughts," my long-time sidekick advised me, "... it's called *free-think*.' Maybe you'll think of something that will get you jump started."

Let it come as no surprise to you that one of my real strong points is not following my wife's suggestions. However, this time I did. For the next three hours I wrote down every thought that crossed my addled and sometimes fevered mind. And, one of the things I discovered is, most of the thoughts that occur to me present themselves in the form of questions.

Another thing I learned is that most of the questions that occur to me don't exactly fall into the deep philosophical category. Most of them in fact are just plain old ordinary everyday questions: pointless, irrelevant, hollow, unrelated and definitely immaterial.

Not so cool, huh?

At any rate, here are a couple of examples. Did you ever wonder about all those people buying stuff on all those TV shopping channels in the middle of the night? Do they actually stay up all night just waiting for the right ring or bracelet to be put on sale?

On an altogether different subject, I started wondering how many times a day I have to get up to let the cat in or out. Our cat (her name is That Damned Cat) never learned to use a litter box. She goes outdoors to do her duty. Judging from the number of times she goes in and out of the house, she either has a lot of duty to do or enjoys watching me open and close doors.

Then I got to wondering about the mole in our front yard. Do you suppose that little sucker is out there now, gnawing his way through the frozen tundra? If he is, he must have teeth as strong as my wife's Uncle Harold's. Uncle Harold looks like a mole and he eats ice.

Here's another thing I think about every now and then. It concerns some of the songs in our hymnal at the Church of Big Miracles. Who sings those hymns? Why are they in our hymnal? Hymnals probably wouldn't be so thick or cost so much if they didn't include all those hymns no one sings and no one but Pastor Good knows.

Another question. How come I always get a cold on Friday night? By Monday I'm usually well enough to go back to work. Sometimes I think I'll get a cold on Monday. That would be weird. Most folks seem to get colds and can't go to work on nice days.

Another question. How come the really neat programs on television are always scheduled after I go to bed? Can't they schedule some of these programs before nine o'clock?

Did you ever notice the commercials about Florida always show lots of sunshine, pristine beaches, and people cavorting in bathing suits? When I go to Florida, it rains, it's cold, and the only thing I see on the beaches is a bunch of bundled up retirees looking for seashells.

And why is it the cable TV company always has line trouble just about the time I'm ready to enjoy my favorite TV show?

Why is it when I find a newspaper that has been left behind in the restaurant, someone has already removed the section I was looking for?

The last note I made to myself was another question. Why is it I spent a whole day thinking about things like this when I could have been taking another nap?

"I've never understood why people go out and rake their lawn before the leaves stop falling. It makes about as much sense as making a pass at your wife while you still got your pants on. By the time you get 'em off she may be out of the mood."
Nelson Algren
What Every Young Man Should Know

In case you haven't noticed, one of the very evident "guy things" is the way we guys like to hurl barbs, affronts, and put downs at each other.

In true curmudgeonly fashion I want to be up front about this quirky bit of male behavior. It's a "guy game."

Men do it and laugh about it. When women try to do it, they sound catty. Men, no matter how crude or cruel, seem to think this kind of stuff is funny. Women, on the other hand, don't seem to grasp this not-so-subtle but always gratifying verbal art form.

So, here, my female column-reading compatriots, are a few aspersions and rebuffs to tuck away in your chatty bag for when they come in handy. I've even provided a handy guide designed to tell you when each is applicable.

To be used on someone stuffy. *"I'll bet you can trace your family tree all the way back to when some of your ancestors lived in one."*

To be used on an uppity aunt, uncle, or former boss. *"Nice dress (or suit). Did you get it new?"*

When a guy hits on you at the bar. *"You know, you remind me of a summer cold. There's no way to get rid of you."*

For use on a former boyfriend. *"My father still thinks you are an angel. He says every time he ever talked to you ... you were harping about something."*

For dismissing a bore. *"You know something, you're a convincing argument for reincarnation. I can tell you were definitely part of a horse in a previous life."*

Assessing bad behavior. *"I'll tell you one thing. If Moses had known someone like you, there would have to have been an eleventh commandment."*

Mild put down (done with a smile). *"I'll bet people who lisp refer to you as a real thinker."*

How to end an argument. *"Look, I refuse to engage in a battle of wits with you. I never argue with someone who isn't armed."*

For someone who is pouting. *"Is that your lower lip or are you wearing a turtleneck?"*

Not so mild put down. *"I think we've met somewhere before. But what the heck, every now and then I have nightmares."*

Thoughtless date (ungentlemanly). *"I'd ask you to be thoughtful but I'll bet you don't do imitations."*

Bizarre or unwarranted behavior. *"I'll bet you are just as happy as if you were in your right mind."*

Oneupsmanship. *"Don't accuse me of making a fool out of you. I don't deserve all the credit."*

Retort to an insult. *"Come, come, now; you're not a perfect fool. No one is perfect."*

Casual put down. *"I'd tell Ripley about you, but I'm sure he would say, 'I don't believe it.'"*

Getting rid of a mooch. *"I'd really like to help you out. Which way did you come in?"*

Telling someone they are off base. *"You know, you're a squirrel's idea of paradise."*

Soft put down. *"I'll bet if you took an aptitude test it would show you are best suited to retirement."*

Work related. *"You know, sending you out to do a man's job is a whole lot like sending a tadpole out to battle a whale."*

To someone acting important. *"I'm impressed. I'll bet you're on the list of the nation's Top Ten Nobodies."*

Employee related. *"I'd gladly pay you what you're worth. But I'd be violating the minimum wage law."*

Put down an egomaniac. *"I'll bet you were voted most

likely to go to seed."

Assessing a disappointing blind date (male). *"You're so homely that even if you were nude riding a horse, the horse would get all the attention."*

Assessing a disappointing blind date (female). *"You remind me of Venus de Milo. Not all there."*

Standard bar room put down. *"Did anyone ever tell you that you have a baby face ... and a brain to match?"*

Standard office water cooler put down. *"Something tells me you were born on April 1."*

Girl to guy. *"If, as they say, ignorance is bliss, you must be delirious."*

Works for either gender. *"I know it's a waste of time to ask you this, but, 'Do you know what?'"*

Know someone who is overly opinionated? *"It would be interesting to know the bias for your opinion."*

Winding up an unwanted conversation. *"I can tell just by talking to you, you aren't the kind to get ulcers. You're the kind that gives them."*

Conversational put down. *"I'll bet you hate know-it-alls. You know, the kind who will occasionally tell you when you're wrong."*

Soft put down. *"You know, I've always said you don't seem to have much on your mind. But today I see you are wearing a hat."*

In a bar. *"If you ever sat down and told me all the things you think about, I'll bet the silence would be unbearable."*

Someone who doesn't get your jokes. *"I gotta admit. You remind me of the guy that invented color radio."*

Okay, ladies, now you know how to communicate with guys. Tear out this little list and go forth, knowing you are armed with ample slams to get you through almost any situation. But if any of the above fail, try this one: Faccia il bagno nel disinfettante se vuol puzzare meno. It's Italian. It means, "Try disinfectant to get rid of your smell." If that doesn't work, tell him, "Ponga las manos en otra parte." In Spanish that means "Keep your greasy hands to yourself."

If neither of those get rid of the guy, tell him to point to his head and abbreviate the mountain. That he should understand.

> "Never eat at a place called Mom's. Never play cards with a man named Doc. And never lie down with a woman who's got more trouble than you."
> Nelson Algren

How physically fit are you?
Think you're about average? About on a par with others

in your age group? Or, maybe you are one of those extremely rare individuals that can exceed the fitness, strength, and flexibility standards for people in your age group.

Why do I bring this up? Because I did a little comparison testing to see how I fared. Would it surprise you if I told you I did pretty well? It would sure surprise me.

The first test was something called "the arm curl test." To perform this test, women need a five-pound weight. Men need an eight-pound weight. I didn't have an eight-pound weight so I decided to use our cat, That Damn Cat. (Actually my daughter gave her cat a name but no one can remember it ... or maybe what we call her now is more appropriate.) At any rate, I used the cat because I estimate her weight to be somewhere between eight and nine pounds. However, as I attempted to lift her up and down in the fashion shown in the illustration, she fought, scratched, struggled, hissed, and howled, finally reducing me to a fit of profanity. With less than marginal success arm curling the cat, I finally resorted to doing the exercise with a box of frozen pizzas.

A person in my age group (that's the "really, really old" age group) is supposed to be able to do this lift and curl exercise 15 times in 30 seconds (that's one "lift and curl" every two seconds for you math challenged readers).

I think I could probably have met the standard but I think I was holding the box of frozen pizzas wrong. Besides, on the fourth lift and curl I hit myself in the nose and got a nosebleed. It took awhile to get the bleeding stopped. By the time I did, I had lost interest in this particular exercise.

Another test was called the "30-second chair stand." At first all I thought I had to do was stand there and watch the chair for 30-seconds. No so. After I read the instructions, I discovered it was a little more complicated (and rigorous) than just standing there.

What you are supposed to do in the 30-second chair stand is sit in the chair with your feet on the floor and arms crossed at your chest. Then you stand up and sit down, stand up and sit down, stand up and sit down. You repeat this little drill for 30 seconds. If you are in your fifties, you should be able to do this 16 times in 30 seconds. If you are in your 70's you should be able to do it about 12 times in 30 seconds.

If you fall somewhere between those two age guidelines, you'll have to do a little interpolating. If you are younger than 50 you shouldn't be reading this essay in the first place. Go read something about how to improve your sex life.

At any rate, based on how many times I was able to perform this little exercise within the allotted time, I would have done rather well providing I was 160 years old.

Before I go any further with my evaluation of these tests, I would like to mention that I feel both of the tests I've described so far are seriously and perhaps even fatally flawed. Nowhere in the arm curling exercise did they tell people not to use a cat. I'm convinced the subsequent loss of blood from cat bites and scratches seriously impacted how well I performed on the arm curl test.

In the second test, the one where you sit down and stand up, the height of the chair has a great deal to do with whether or not a person can perform to some predetermined standard. Example: If you only had to lift your body up a couple of inches like you would be required to do if you were sitting on a bar stool, it wouldn't be so difficult (at least not for awhile). On the other hand, if you were sitting on a little bitty person's potty training chair, it would be far more difficult throughout the exercise. That's why I say, in order for a test to be valid, it has to be standardized.

There was another test called the "eight foot up and go test." In this test you had to sit in a chair, stand up, walk eight feet, turn around, return to your chair and then sit down again.

The Curmudgeon Rides Again

Doesn't sound too tough, does it?

This test is supposed to simulate getting up, going and getting something from another room, and then returning to where you were originally sitting. The tester indicated how many times individuals of varying ages were supposed to be able to do the exercise in a specified amount of time, but I won't go into all of that. Suffice to say, however, this test is also seriously flawed.

What does this test sound like to you? You're right. It very definitely sounds like a wife, mother, or grandmother getting up from a breakfast (or lunch, or dinner) table, going and getting something for some member of the family, and then returning to the table to continue eating.

Let me point out. This is not a fair test. This is not a standardized test. That's because women do this all the time. Which is another way of saying they are in much better condition to handle this particular maneuver and hence be very good at this test.

Men, on the other hand, are not likely to do well in this particular exercise. Men have always had someone go get the tools they need when they are performing little chores around the house. Plus, men are rendered even further out of condition to perform exercises of this nature as the result of their continued control of the television remote.

I would like to point out, however, that I did pass one of the tests in the series. It's called "the walking test." Moonbeam, however, disputes this claim. She says I cannot take credit for walking. She claims our dog, Freight Train, drags me.

> "The average man's opinions would be much less foolish if he would learn to think for himself."
> Bertrand Russell
> *Sceptical Essays*, 1928

I received a letter the other day. The lady had just finished reading one of my earlier novels, *Pagoda*. "When did you quit writing 'spooky stories?'" she wanted to know.

Answer: When my publisher told me to. Stephen King has that market tied up.

Nevertheless, because the nature of my first 10 novels or so were along the "spooky" line, whenever I do a writer's conference or speaking engagement, people always seem to ask me if I believe in the "supernatural."

To be honest (I seldom am), I don't know what I believe about the anomalistic or hyperphysical. Even so, I can tell you this much, a good many of the people I have interviewed in the process of doing research for a particular "spooky" book believe very strongly that their lives have been impacted or influenced by "other realm forces."

In one of my early books I wanted to develop a character who had an "out of body" or "near death" experience. In an attempt to get a feel for what an "out of body" experience was like, I asked some of my friends if they knew anyone who claimed to have been through such a happening.

Before long I was getting phone calls ... lots of calls. People volunteered. Curiously enough, each of them had one proviso – no names. They were adamant enough about the "no names" bit that I was reasonably certain I wasn't satisfying someone's need for a little publicity.

Even more curious than the insistence on anonymity was the fact that each of them, during the course of the interview, related a similar set of circumstances. Note I said similar. They were clearly not identical.

We have all heard about, and some of you out there may even know, people who claim to have died and left their body for some period of time. Then, for some reason came back.

Most of us have heard what they say they "lived through" (no pun intended ... but you will admit it is a curious choice of words) during the occurrence.

Mind stretching? Credibility stretching? Who knows?

Someone asked me once if I believed I had ever had an "out of body experience." I told the person, "No." Hey, gang, get real. If I had one, I certainly would not have come back in the same short, fat body I had just managed to get out of.

Okay, you say, what about ghosts? Do ghosts exist? Do they hang around and haunt places (houses, old castles, gay bars)? Who knows? At the same time I will admit several of my early books were written around scary characters such as demons, devils, hobgoblins and former bosses.

It should come as no surprise to you that even those characters carved out of the spirit world have to be researched. And, it should come as no surprise to you that I got a surprising number of responses to my request for people who claim to have witnessed a haunting or encountered a ghost.

Once again I got the "no names" stipulation. But I can tell you that the two strangest (and most bizarre) stories came from a local "man of the cloth" and a bank officer. Each gave me a disturbing version of their somewhat brief encounter with "other world forces."

Did I believe them? Yes and no and no and yes. I'm

convinced they believed what they were telling me. I will tell you this much though; I don't know how I would have handled it if I had been through the same experience. In truth though, if I had lived through what they claim they did, they probably would have shipped me back to the cookie factory by now for repackaging.

Out-of-body experiences and encounters with ghosts aren't the only thing I have dealt with in some of my books. In one book, entitled *Ancients*, published and released back in the late 1980's, I built the story around a Big Foot type of character. When the book came out, several people called me wanting to know if I had ever had an encounter with a Big Foot type character.

The answer in this case is an unequivocal — yes. Mabel Strap had the biggest feet of any girl I ever dated. Friends warned me that if I started dating her and ended up taking her to a dance, I was endangering life and limb. She stepped on Garth Boykal's foot once at a dance, broke three of his toes, and ended his career as the best punter on the football team. I can't verify this but I am told the local Girl Scout troop used to invite her to campfires to put the fire out when they were through roasting marshmallows.

Just as much as "out of body" experiences, ghosts and strange creatures, people were always reciting stories about flying saucers. People like to talk about Area 51 in Nevada. I have to confess, when I go to Nevada, I don't go to Area 51. I go to Las Vegas. That's when I see "other realm creatures." But most of them are playing one-armed bandits.

Bottom line: I've never had what some folks call a "close encounter" (unless you want to call the time I passed Sharon Stone in the Los Angeles air terminal a close encounter). But, to be honest with you, I don't think that's what the folks I talk to are talking about. When they tell me about their "close encounters" they say space aliens take people up into their spaceship and perform a whole battery of tests on them.

The Curmudgeon Rides Again

Okay, if you are the investigative type, I know what your next question is going to be. You want to know what kind of tests, right?

I look at it this way ... surely they would want "unusual" people. And I'm certain they would want to give these people all kinds of tests: a spelling test, a urine test, and maybe even a little exercise to determine if any of them are bed-wetters.

In any case, if any of you out there run into some folks from an alien spaceship and they tell you they need an unusual specimen or two. Tell them to contact me. My family is peopled with characters that would fit their requirements.

One Last Thought

"I promise to keep on living as though I expected to live forever. Nobody grows old by merely living a number of years. People grow old only by deserting their ideals. Years may wrinkle the skin, but to give up your interests and your passions ... that wrinkles the soul."
Douglas MacArthur
New York Times, 1984

If you have had the misfortune to know a writer, or worse yet, been saddled with one in the family, you know that an essay is never finished, a book never done. Give a writer the opportunity and he will revise what he has written ten times ten.

I never knew a writer (wordsmith, pen pusher, playwright, journalist, scribe, or mythmaker) who was truly satisfied with what

The Curmudgeon Rides Again

he had written when the effort was "finished."

If I happen, as I sometimes do, to rifle through the pages of a novel I wrote fifteen years ago, or a column I wrote seven years ago, I see endless possibilities to improve upon what I have written. But, if I gave in to that impulse to change one more word, rearrange one more sentence, shorten one more paragraph, I would have missed a dozen or more deadlines. Missing deadlines is a no no.

An individual who has the opportunity to write and have people read what he has written each week is fortunate. By now you know that I have a great affection for the wit and wisdom contained in the dozen or so books of quotations I have been fortunate to spend time with. I am also extremely fond of humor. An evening spent thumbing through books by Henny Youngman, Lenny Bruce, and others of their generation, to me, is extremely rewarding. I laugh a lot. Laughter is good.

So, read on. One more quotation (author unknown) and one more column. Sorry, I couldn't resist.

One Last Thought

"It's never as bad as you thought it would be. It's never as good as you hoped it would be."
Author unknown

A lady recently sent me a copy of a letter she received from her grandmother, age 85. In it, the charming lady carefully outlined what she would do differently if she were given the opportunity to live her life over.

The list, as she wrote it, is thought provoking and touching. For example, she said if she had it to do over, she would ride more merry-go-rounds, pick more flowers, and eat more ice cream. She also said she wouldn't eat so many things she didn't like just because "they were good for her."

My favorite, though, was when she said, "If I had it to do all over again, I would just plain take things less seriously."

Hey, I haven't exactly arrived at that stage of my life when I'm ready to wrap up things and put a bow around my earthly activities. But needless to say, what this 85-year-old woman had to say got me to thinking. I believe in what Douglas MacArthur had to say, " ... the soul wrinkles" if you do that. But (Isn't there always a "but?") I can identify some of the changes I would make if I did have it to do over.

The first change I would make would take me all the way back to my grade school years. I think the good nuns at Saint Paul might have looked at me with a bit more charity if I always hadn't been the kind of kid I was. Still, I'll maintain to my dying day that Sister Arnulfa was just plain nasty (picture Darth Vader in a nun's habit). With her it was unfettered guerrilla warfare.

The Curmudgeon Rides Again

Once I put cat-eye marbles in her soup. I was kinda hoping she would swallow one. But she discovered the marbles before that happened.

She looked straight at me and I confessed. I told her I saw David Mennsing do it. David had to stay in at recess for two whole weeks. I told David I thought it was too bad someone squealed on him and he got caught.

Then there was the time Bernard Goldman and I put the dead carp in the school's central ventilation system. Boy, did that stink. Sister Arnulfa said it made her sick to her stomach. They had to fumigate the school. I was a hero. We didn't have to go to school for two whole days.

I imagine it's hard for some of you folks out there to appreciate the intensity of my ongoing battles with Sister Arnulfa. When she passed me from the fifth to the sixth grade, she probably thought she was rid of me. But when I came back to school that fall the administration assigned her to the sixth grade and we went at it again.

Some people have no luck.

Two straight years of doing battle with Sister Arnulfa made a lasting impression on me. When I went into the Air Force, I had to undergo psychological testing because I told the base shrink I was having a recurrent nightmare about being attacked by a giant German penguin.

Ultimately, though, I won the head game with Sister Arnulfa. When I wrote my third novel, *Pagoda*, I had the fifth grade boy in my story lock his teacher (guess what her name was) in the basement of the old school and feed her to the giant slugs.

Victory, victory, that's our cry ...

Another thing I would do differently back in my school years would be the classes I took. First of all, I would not take three years of Latin again. What a waste that was. Sister Arnulfa

One Last Thought

told me that if I took enough Latin I could read what the doctor was writing on that little prescription pad of his. What a crock. Three years of conjugating verbs and I still can't read what the doctor is writing. Why wasn't someone pounding on the doctor to take penmanship lessons?

Another thing I would change about those days has to do with Mardela Krink. If I had any idea how wealthy her dad was, I wouldn't have been so standoffish when she asked me to the Sadie Hawkins Day dance. The rumor around school was that Mardela liked fat boys, and I was her number one choice.

When I turned her down, she asked Bernard Goldman (he of dead carp fame) to go to the dance with her. Bernard accepted. They arrived at Precious Blood in Mardela's brand new Studebaker, and I was kinda sorry I turned her down. I never did get to ride in a brand new Studebaker.

Actually, there is a lot more I'd like to change, but I think I better get some of those early years cleaned up first.

9 780964 560642